Step Up!

THOMAS DOLD

STEP UP!

THE ULTIMATE STAIR RUNNING TRAINING BOOK

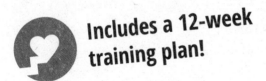 Includes a 12-week training plan!

TECHNIQUE • TRAINING • MOTIVATION

Meyer & Meyer Sport

British Library of Cataloguing in Publication Data
A catalogue record for this book is available from the British Library

Original title: *Step Up: Trainingsbuch Treppenlaufen*, © 2023 by Meyer & Meyer Verlag

Step Up
Maidenhead: Meyer & Meyer Sport (UK) Ltd., 2024
ISBN: 978-1-78255-268-0

© 2024 by Meyer & Meyer Sport (UK) Ltd.
Aachen, Auckland, Beirut, Cairo, Cape Town, Dubai, Hägendorf, Hong Kong, Indianapolis, Maidenhead, Manila, New Delhi, Singapore, Sydney, Tehran, Vienna
Member of the World Sport Publishers' Association (WSPA), www.w-s-p-a.org

Printed by Versa Press, East Peoria, IL
Printed in the United States of America

ISBN 978-1-78255-268-0
Email: info@m-m-sports.com
www.thesportpublisher.com

CONTENTS

INTRODUCTION

Welcome! I'm glad that you are here and that we have the chance to step up together. There are many ways to do this and stairs are one of the most common and easiest ways to get to the top.

Whether in the department store, at home, or on the winner's podium, stairs are everywhere. Have you ever wondered how to make use of this constantly available fitness tool? This book is for you if you're interested in any of the following:

+ Stair running as a competitive sport for real achievers

+ Stair training as complementary training for other sports

+ Stair running as a way to increase your fitness in general

If none of these catch your eye or if you would prefer to be on the couch, you will still be interested in the entertaining stories from the tower-running circus and the chapter on focus and mental training.

About the Author

After a 20-year career in competitive sports, including 45 international stair running victories—seven in a row at the Empire State Building Run Up—and world records and world championship titles in backward running, a list of my accomplishments would take up several pages. If you would like to see the individual races and world records, they can be found at *www.erfolge.thomasdold.com.*

Crossing the finish line on the helipad at the China World Summit Wing in Beijing. Winning the Empire State Building Run Up.

I started playing soccer when I was seven years old, but transitioned first to running at the age of 17 and, a short time later, to mountain running. Winning the bronze medal for Germany with the junior team at the 2002 World Mountain Running Championships was the first important highlight of my running career.

In 2003 I began my stair-running career at the Donauturm in Vienna. It took two years of intensive training and many stair-running sessions before I was fit enough to win tower runs, but ever since then I have traveled to taller and taller buildings around the world (in whose emergency staircases competitions are held). In addition to my sporting successes—the world records, the world championship titles, the trophies—these experiences and people I have met along the way have shaped my personality.

Over the years, not only has the world changed, so, too, have stair running and, particularly, myself. My personal journey has taken me from a young, inexperienced athlete hungry for success to one with more to offer than the mindset of a serial winner who achieves every goal with iron discipline and steely will.

It is possible to take a relaxed approach to physical and mental training and exercises. Top performance without gritted teeth has many advantages!

> I love hearing from people—often after I have been a guest on a talk show—who say that now they take the stairs much more often and are having fun doing it. You're alone on the winner's podium, but moving forward together is a different kind of reward. Who are you willing to have fun with on the stairs, sweating after flights and flights of exercises?

How the Book Is Structured

Anyone can walk or run up stairs. But at train stations and airports, you quickly notice who is confident on the stairs and using the handrail and who is untrained.

To get you started, we look at the positive effects of taking and running stairs. In the following section, you get an overview of the topic of stair running. After that we will start with the basic elements like step technique, use of handrails, and so on in more detail. Explanations on using training areas and training methods will ensure a healthy and long-term ascent.

Once you have sufficient basics and tips for your training strategy, you will learn practical exercises for different fitness levels. In addition to stair running for beginners and advanced athletes, chapter 9 provides many ideas and inspiration for trainers and athletes from other sports who want to improve their training.

Each exercise has been rated on a scale of one to three stars with three stars representing the most challenging exercises.

Coordination and strengthening exercises on the stairs can be challenging. But the goal is not to inspire the next world champion tower runner. That is why the 12-week training plans are designed for beginners, amateurs, and ambitious runners. In addition, there are tips and tricks on special equipment and national and international competitions.

Mental preparation and resilience are key to stair running and therefore an entire chapter has been dedicated to these topics (see chapter 19).

WARM-UP

For many people, the thought of running up a skyscraper at a sprint pace may seem intimidating. It's a feeling I can't dismiss out of hand; even after 45 tower running victories on five continents, the thought is true, the impression is real.

1.1   Why Stair Running?

- Why do thousands of people of all fitness levels still take the exhausting way up to the observation platforms of these prestigious buildings? Why do they insist on going on foot when high-tech elevators are waiting nearby?

This question about the WHY is clarified in this book as well as the question about the HOW. This will give you a sense of how taking more steps in your life can lead you to rise higher. You'll recognize the opportunities that the oft-avoided fitness devices give you everywhere—in cities in high-rise buildings and as a natural staircase in vineyards and hillsides in rural areas.

1.2 Perspective and Approach

This is the second focus of the book. Stair running challenges the body—if you want it to. However, there are valid reasons why stair running is often not included in training by many runners, endurance athletes, and athletes in general. The reasons lie in the approach, and that is the second point to which the book is dedicated.

There are objective and subjective reasons why someone takes the elevator or the stairs, why someone wins competitions and why someone else comes in second. Rarely are the physical reasons the real cause. The stairs of this world therefore offer not only the possibilities to strengthen the body, but also, for those who wish, to train the mind. Chapter 19 will discuss how to use this mental training in your everyday life.

1.3   After Each Stair Run Comes the Descent

Wherever you are in the world, no stair climber has ever remained on the observation platform; for all of them, the ascent is followed by the descent. This metaphor describes life. It is a constant alternation between two polarities—tension and relaxation, ascent and descent, health and sickness, and the most extreme contrast between life and death. Nothing remains, not even physical performance; everything is subject to a constant rising and passing away.

These experiences and this mindset flow into this book as well as my experiences as a trainer of beginner, amateur, and internationally successful professional athletes who compete in the Olympic Games.

I know from painful experience: no trophy, no victory, and no goal achieved can really make you happy. The relief behind the finish line, the recognition, and attention are wonderful. But that is not happiness, it is like salt water when you are thirsty. Being happy takes place within you, in silence and stillness. With all the variety of experiences and knowledge, the focus of this book—the exercises and knowledge transfer—is on you. YOU should have fun while reading and especially during practicing and through this achieving your goals. In this sense, there is a short warm-up and then we'll start with the core content. If you are very impatient, you can start directly with the practical exercises; you can always read the theory and tips on technique and training later.

WHY RUNNING STAIRS?

Usually you ask yourself the question of WHY at the very beginning.

• Why you have picked up this book and why are you are interested in exploring stair running?

Wherever this interest comes from, the main thing is that it leads to action and to trying it out in practice. If in the last days, weeks, months, and years you have not yet broken a sweat by running and climbing stairs, and your running shirt is still fresh and clean in your closet, this chapter will help you recognize the benefits of stair running.

If you have absolutely no intrinsic motivation for stair running, you can read as much as you want about the benefits; at any given moment, you will come up with a thousand excuses why climbing stairs is not for you right now. I have experienced this for 20 years and I know all the excuses people make for themselves, me, and others.

But you seem to have a flame of interest and motivation in you and we will keep it fueled with objective arguments until the stair running fire is big enough to fuel you.

2.1   Fun Factor and Attractiveness

- Many of my seminar participants wonder:

- How can running stairs be fun?

- Aren't the stairwells musty and dark?

- Isn't the climb exhausting?

That's exactly the thrill, the motivation. If you're really hungry, you look forward to eating. A warm sunbath seems especially beautiful in dreary, dark, rainy weather in February. The power and sensations you feel as you run up the stairwell and finally reach the top cannot be described in words. The hormone cocktail that the body gives you as a reward is particularly long-lasting, usually for hours or even the whole day. The investment for this is the devotion to the stairs.

Those who are more committed to pushing the physical and mental boundaries will be exuberantly rewarded. This reward consists of an expanded physical and mental freedom. On the one hand, through the physical adjustment after supercompensation and on the other, through a new awareness of what you can handle.

How strong these effects and feelings are is up to you. It is true: Everything becomes simultaneously more intense; a momentum develops that every athlete knows. Often unconsciously the body and mind want to experience this feeling again; this turns on the staircase magnet and sets this (positive) devil's cycle in motion. You now know that after overcoming the initial resistance, your stair running will take off. Let's go.

2.2   Challenge Yourself

For all competitors who love accuracy, comparability, and measurability, stair running is the Mecca. In the stairwells of the world, there is no wind and no bad weather—at least for indoor stair running. Outdoors, in the vineyards, for example, things are different, of course.

Because the external parameters are very constant, you can measure up—with others or, and this is a special mental challenge, with yourself. Look at and train with the stopwatch on your arm, the hammering pulse in your throat, the limits of what is possible with your body. You can compare a workout from last year, last month, or last week with your current workout, and you'll know immediately how well you're doing right now. With the exception of you and your performance, everything in the stairwell stays pretty constant.

This is not everyone's cup of tea and some people break out in a sweat just reading about it. But always remember: In each of us there is a winner and the challenge gene. We see it in small children, but in many adults it has faded so much that it has become invisible. However, this gene is built into each body and can be awakened.

If you feel it right now, put the book aside and go for a run. The book can wait; your thighs, your calves, and your anticipation of the steps want to experience the feeling.

2.3   Variety

Stability and variety need a suitable ratio. Experiencing the same food and drink every day is rarely a desirable goal. That is why effective training consists of basic training and sessions that alternate over and over again. Here, stairs can be a special splash of color in the training gray. Especially in winter, when the weather outside makes intensive sessions difficult, it is often shorts weather in the stairwell. The diversity of each staircase also creates variety. Whether it's the handrail on the left or right, the height and depth of the steps, the overall ascent, and of course whether the staircase turns clockwise or counterclockwise.

"Climbing stairs has gone from a chore to a joyful challenge, and my thoughts wander to you ... It was nice hearing from you!"

–Feedback from a participant after a stair-running seminar

These are just a few of the obvious parameters that add variety to running stairs. Add to this your own physical shape, because with a higher level of fitness you will experience a completely different running sensation in the same staircase. Fighting against each step becomes like flying on an inclined plane towards the sky. This will certainly take a few thousand steps of training, but at least for a few floors almost everyone can feel this feeling of lightness and of flying towards the sky.

2.4 Training Stimuli

"I run six times a week and I'm not getting any better!"
—Quote from a running seminar participant

In conversation, she explained that every morning, except Sunday, she and her friend jog the same loop, chatting or just running quietly next to each other. It usually takes them the same amount of time to complete the loop. If you don't put your body out of balance (homeostasis), you won't feel any adaptation. The physical performance increase can only happen if you move outside of the performance range you have been used to. Then the complex process of increasing the load tolerance will be set in motion and sooner or later you will notice more power and more endurance!

Stair running is a very intensive load, which is almost always outside the normal load balance. Therefore there are some important aspects to consider so that you do not strain your body. Stair running is excellent for friends of high-intensity interval training (HIIT).

2.5 Mental Training

Many tower runs take place in staircases without windows and the entertainment of nature or spectators. This challenges your mental strength, because you will only be motivated from within for the next step. Due to the high load and effort, mental training is of particular importance. That's why there is a separate chapter that also covers the topics of focus, goals, and setbacks.

2.6 Constant Training Conditions

Many stairs are reserved exclusively for you. Whether in high-rise buildings or in nature, on the stairs you have a high chance to train undisturbed. No soccer team accidentally shoots balls at you, no trucks cross your path, and no cyclists overtake you. On the stairs you can do your training. This creates constant training conditions.

2.7 Extraordinary Competitions

For my stair-running colleague Matthias Jahn, with whom I competed for many years in the worldwide competitions, that was the spark that lit the fire. When I told him I was running up the world's tallest building in Taiwan, a switch flipped in him. From then on, he, and at times we together, trained for the stair races in the metropolises.

Doing sports in the centers of the world's cities is a unique selling point. The view after the race is indescribable. Of course, not everyone who reads the book will be in New York to run up the Empire State Building, but perhaps the Millennium Tower in Vienna or the Swissotel in Singapore is worth a trip?

Maybe this is how your journey starts, into a whole new world—that of staircases, mega-cities, high performance, and training optimization.

Tower run in Ho Chi Minh City, Vietnam at the Bitexco Financial Tower.

3 GETTING STARTED: HOW DO YOU RUN STAIRS IN EVERYDAY LIFE?

Climbing stairs is easy! One foot in front of the other, step by step, until you reach the top. For everyday life, this approach is sufficient. It does not matter whether the handrail is used, how the turnings are made on the landings, and where the gaze is directed.

For those who want to know more about what can be experienced, this section provides the basic knowledge. The basics of the technique are presented in such a way that they are directly applicable for practical use. Because that is the goal: that you feel comfortable and at home on the stairs of this world.

Never take the elevator or escalator again?

That's an honorable goal, but from my own experience, it's not achievable. In buildings, especially the very high ones, it is impossible to take the stairs to the very top. Access to the observation decks, offices, and upper department store floors is often via the "easy" way with escalators and elevators.

This does not seem tragic, however, because there are plenty of other opportunities to take the stairs in the world.

3.1 Your Attitude and Approach to Stairs

Friends have often said, "Boy, that must be really strenuous!" when they hear about training or competitions. Everyone has experienced how strenuous it is to climb stairs. One of the noticeable signs is the pulse, which after a few steps and floors begins to beat in the body.

If you bought the book yourself, you are very likely one of the people who see stairs at least as a possible workout and a tool for their own fitness. With this basic mindset that their use is donated exercise time, burns extra calories, strengthens the muscles, makes the heart beat faster, and much more, the stairs transform from a sweaty bugbear to an ever-present personal trainer who always has a few steps ready for you.

3.2 View Direction

In addition to observing the staircase or the surroundings, it is particularly—useful especially at the beginning—to look at the stairs.

• Are they uneven?

• How deep is each one?

• What is the surface like?

• Are they rough, slippery, or grippy?

Steps are different. Indoors, you can assume that the steps won't change much. Outside, and especially in the nature, stairs can be very irregular. The view should then be directed more to the steps than to the surroundings in order to move forward without stumbling (e.g., the next 5-10 steps in between looking at the next landing). This way you get a feeling of what is coming and where to place the next step. The best thing is to try it out, and find which angle suits you best.

3.3 Step Technique

Usually people take one step at a time. That means, with each step, one overcomes a step. The right foot climbs up to the next step, the left foot foot overtakes the right foot and is placed one step higher than the previous right foot set. This sounds more complicated in theory than it is in practice.

For particularly narrow staircases or if the steps are unusual, for example at an airy height, it is possible to place the rear foot on the same step. For example, you climb with your right foot and place your left foot next to it.

If you have a handrail handy, you can use this as a support. Sometimes it is better not to use the railing (e.g., it is very high or low) or quite pragmatically, when your hands are already full with shopping bags.

The steps in the 48 m high tower of the Ambuluwawa temple in Sri Lanka are sometimes less than 30 cm wide. Overtaking is almost impossible—and yet unavoidable, since there is only one staircase.

3.4 Helpful Strength Exercises

You don't need special strengthening exercises for normal everyday stair climbing. Why would you? Everyone walks up and down stairs. But if you take the stairs more often and more intensively, you will notice how much strain is placed on your calves. Therefore it is a good idea to do a stretching and strengthening exercise.

3.5 Calf Lift

Starting position:

Stand with the front part of your foot on the edge of the first step; only the balls of your feet touch the step, the heels are in the air and protrude beyond the edge of the step.

Exercise description:

Press up on your toes and hold the position at the highest point for 1-2 seconds. Then lower the heels as far as possible, preferably to below the edge of the step until you feel a stretch in the calves.

Reps: 3-10 times

Rest: one minute between reps

Sets: 2-3 times

Strong training effect: calves

VARIATION:

The exercise is easier if you hold on to a wall or handrail. This is a strengthening exercise with an integrated stretching element. Many more strengthening, stretching, and coordination exercises can be found in the corresponding chapters of the book.

Two-leg calf lift

Variation: One-leg calf lift

4 ASCENT: STAIR RUNNING AT FULL POWER

On your marks!

This is how every race up the Empire State Building started, followed by the deafening noise of the horn. What then ran for a good 10 minutes as an automatic program in body and mind was the result of thousands of hours of practice. It looks so easy on TV, but what's behind it?

4.1 Mindset and Attitude at Full Speed

It is different for every runner, but there are commonalities.

1. Think about the goal

If you know at the start what you are running for, you are ahead of the game. Whoever does not forget the goal in the meantime will reach the finish—and perhaps his own goal. Whoever is preoccupied with the aches and pains of the race, the imponderables of the ascent, and the difficulties of the external factors will lose concentration and therefore stop focusing on the finish and his own goal. Learn more about this in chapter 20 with instructions for and practical examples of practice.

2. Unconditionality

There are a thousand reasons to stop and give up in a tower run (and in everything in life). The question that arises:

- Why give up or continue?

It's no different in the stairwell, and the question is loud and pressing.

- Why am I doing this to myself?
- Why didn't I stay at home?
- Why?

There is hardly any escape from this endless circle of pointless questioning. Question after question, the energy is directed in a way that does not lead to the goal. That is why I have always answered this question in advance:

- Why? Because I have decided it.
- Why am I here? Because I have decided it.
- Why does it hurt so much? Because I am ready to give everything.
- Why am I not at home? Because I have made up my mind.
- Why am I doing this to myself? Because I've decided to do it.
- Why am I not running a little slower? Because I have chosen to do this. Because I have chosen this unconditionality.

It may sound a bit intense, but it has pulled my body and mind from the edge of collapse in many races. Why? Because that was my limit to which I ran. It was about testing limits, and the slogan dictated the pace: nothing is impossible.

At the time, there was no alternative to this strategy for me. Today I can offer you an alternative, because not everyone wants to maltreat their body and mind in order to to be a few seconds faster at the finish line. Besides, it is not possible for every brain to live with such an unconditional will. Learn more about this in chapter 19.

4.2   View Direction

How the track looks, where the curve is, and where the railing is are all important elements for arriving quickly, successfully, and without injury at the finish on the observation platforms. It helps to focus exactly on the steps and the handrail at the beginning. After a few floors, it is ideal if you have internalized the rhythm of the stairs; look ahead and scan entire flights of stairs. One look just to make sure everything is okay, just like the last set of stairs. This saves focus power and allows you to concentrate on other things.

It's best to keep your eyes straight ahead and to not hang your head. You can tell from the common saying that it's good to keep your head upright. By looking ahead, you'll be more powerful and light-footed on the steps.

Another trick is to look ahead at the turns or landings; direct your eyes toward the coming landing and your body will run toward this focus point. Visually fixing the steps and handrail at the point where you want to run helps you move forward.

4.3 Stair Technique

Step by step towards the goal; anyone can and does run stairs. But anyone who has ever stood in front of 1,000 or more steps will soon be confronted with the question: How am I supposed to do that?

And the saying "Anyone can do it" is only of limited help; it is too superficial. Even if it seems trivial, running stairs is technically and coordinatively demanding and increases with increasing speed. The layman notices this when he wants to copy the professionals. There is a difference.

4.4 2-2 Technique for Winners

How many steps do you take per step? I have answered this question a thousand times. Take two is the worldwide credo for winning tower runs.

With 3-4 steps per second as the average speed, the ascent in the professional men's field is too fast to touch every step. The frequency is too high for one to sustain it. This would be similar to riding in the Tour de France with a small chainring and the riders pedaling rapidly for hours like they are in spin class. That's inefficient. The stair running version of a large chainring is two steps per step.

Few in the world run this technique for a complete race. Until 2009, the *Taipei 101* was the tallest building in the world, with 508 meters to the top, 390 meters in height, 2,046 steps, and 91 floors in the stair race. There it is usually only the winner who keeps up the two-step technique; the other 5,000 runners manage their techniques differently.

4.5 1-1 Technique

Each step is touched with a frequency as high as possible as you climb up the stairwell. When you try it, you will notice that this technique works well and easily. Also you will feel that it is a somewhat choppy movement, compared to the technique of taking two steps at a time.

With the 1-1 technique, you can still move forward very quickly, power out, and run toward your goals high up on buildings and towers. Because you need less maximum strength to do this, it's the main technique for women in the tall buildings, whether you're aiming for top ten finishes or are a leisure runner.

The downside to this is that it's not quite a fluid movement, and the feeling of flying on an inclined plane does not occur. If you want that feeling, you can test the 2-2 technique on short sections and feel the difference and then apply the following 1-2 technique.

4.6   1-2 Technique

This is the combination of the two techniques. You start with two steps per step and later take each step separately, then go back to two steps per step. This way you can vary the effort and make it ideal for you. The muscles are stimulated in different ways, between a varied focus on speed and strength.

The change of technique has an additional coordinative component, especially for non-stair runners (e.g., from game sports). This is increased by changing the technique on each floor or even on each landing. The constant change of rhythm will be familiar to game athletes and provides an additional mental training stimulus.

4.7   Weight Shift

The body automatically shifts the weight when it comes to the turns on the platforms. The upper body leans in toward the handrail and the turn is made more easily. In very narrow stairwells (e.g., in the Hotel *Park Inn* at Alexanderplatz in Berlin) mirrored movement is also possible. With outstretched arms and a slight shift of the body's center of gravity toward the outer wall, you can easily push off the wall to make the turn. In addition to shifting your weight inward and outward, shifting your weight forward and backward is helpful on flat sections.

On the steps, most runners have a slight upper body forward lean (i.e., a small bend in the hips). This changes the workload ratio from the calf and core muscles toward greater use of the thigh muscles. On flat sections (e.g., when changing staircases or when you want to sprint away flat after the stairs at the top of the observation deck, helipad), you then need to shift your weight backwards, making your running style more upright and stretching your (lumbar) spine. This makes it easier for you to achieve longer stride lengths and run faster.

If you have a few meters or a few hundred meters of run-up to the first step, you should then reverse the posture sequence. Stay as upright as possible on the flat part and arrive at the steps with a feeling of: "I'm running into the stairs" and initiate a slight forward lean of the upper body.

4.8 Foot Placement

The two questions I hear most often are:

- Where do you place your foot?
- How do you place your foot?

The answer here is what everyone will feel during the practical test: The fore/midfoot is the best option. Stepping onto a flat foot or the heel makes the running slow, sluggish, and heavy, because the preload in the foot is missing.

By taking a step up, you will notice the important role the calf muscles play in stair running. They generate the power that springs you upward from the ankle. This effect depends, of course, on the level of training, but try to experience and take advantage of this effect by placing your foot on the step and giving an upward impulse like a small spring.

> **Note for game athletes:** If you manage to spring loosely on steep stairs, you will also have an easier time on the soccer field or tennis court.

The foot should be placed on the step from the top if possible. Pushing into the step does not make sense because of the resistance of the soles (figure 3) and because the preload created by the foot contact from above does not occur.

The foot is best placed in the middle part of the step (figure 1), but if the steps are very narrow, there is no alternative but to place the foot at the very front (figure 2), directly where the vertical section of the preliminary step comes down.

4.9 Using the Handrail

One of the most famous mountain runners and 10,000-meter Olympians did not always use the handrail during his starts on the stairs. Jonathan Wyatt (New Zealand) dominated mountain running like no other at the beginning of the millennium. At times he won more than one race, preferably mountain races, in one weekend and often with a course record.

At the *Taipei 101 Run-Up*, he had a 60-second lead which lasted until floor 50—when I overtook him. Without using the handrail and with a 1-1 technique, he had no chance at winning the competition and achieving a fast time that day.

So why should you use the handrail and what is the most effective way to do it?

Full-body effort: pushing off the wall with one hand and pulling on the railing with the other.

Usually when you run, it's in a fluid motion in the same direction all the time. However, with running stairs, on each landing you change the running direction by 180 degrees. You can regain that feeling of fluid motion by using the handrail and swinging your arm and hand around the landing.

Describing the technique in words is not easy; because a picture is worth a thousand words, here is a series of pictures to demonstrate the arm motion.

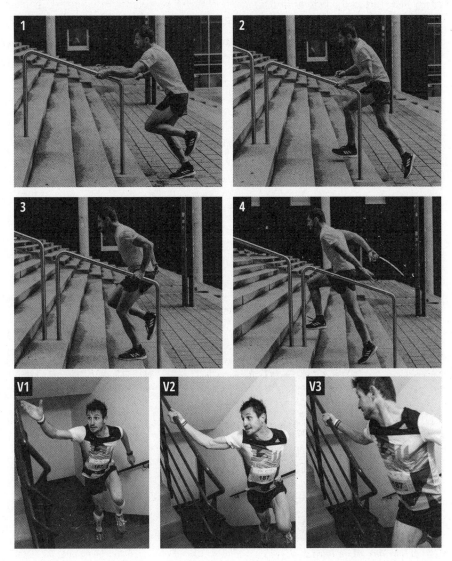

4.10 Overtaking

It is not easy to move ahead one position in a mass start race; overtaking is as difficult on the stairs as it is on the landings. You have to take the long way around the outside of the turn. Although there are probably countless unfair ways to overtake an opponent, I've rarely encountered it and have instead experienced a lot of fair overtaking.

At my first start at the *Empire State Building Run-Up*, I was on the 74th floor—12 floors before the finish—when I let the Austrian Rudolf Reitberger run past on the inside at the handrail. He was faster at that moment. But only at that moment. Once he was in front of me, he didn't run any further away. We crossed the finish line at the same time in the closest final of all time—he as the winner, I in second place. It can be so easy to overtake, even in the most important tower run in the world.

I experienced something similar at the stair race in Chongqing with Piotr Lobodzinski in 2014. While he had won the race in Beijing seven days earlier, my legs were better in the former capital of China. After the mass start he was in sight and let me pass on floor 45, when I wanted to and could run faster, so that after 72 floors there were 28 seconds between us.

Start in New York: At the mass start, everyone fights for a good position before going onto the steps.

In doing so, I ran and overtook in the way I prefer to do. Run to the other runner, touch him on the handrail to ask him to run faster. After a few floors over the limit—the other runner knocked out and with a hammering pulse—overtaking is much easier. I have often heard from other runners that the change of position was lot of uselessly consumed energy.

But most often everyone runs his own race. In single starts (e.g., with 30 seconds distance between runners), you don't meet any other runner on the way. The runners are sorted and ranked according to performance classes, usually starting with the fastest. If one or more runners are caught up, the difference in speed is so big that overtaking is easy. A short, clear call and fair play in the stairwell enables the further brisk ascent. The same applies of course, if one is overtaken oneself.

4.11 Tactics

The famous race up the Empire State Building had a big mass start until 2012. After that, the field was reduced to 20–30 elite athletes. Divided into two groups of men and one group of women, there have been three starting blocks for the 300 participants. The first group of men lined up at the front in order based on the previous year's rankings. When nine runners are lined up next to each other and a total of 130 men are lined up behind each other, you can easily imagine the crowd at the entrance door after a 10-meter sprint.

In mass starts, it is important to start running as fast as possible. However, if you think that you can win a race based on the first meters and floors, you will lose everything at the end. The race is decided in the second half and very often even in the last floors. That is why after the fast start and the first few fast floors, you enter the middle section of the race where it settles into a rhythm, which is at the performance limit, the runners panting floor by floor.

Those who have no ambition for winner's trophies can still take advantage of the tactic and, as in a city marathon, try to run both halves of the race as fast as possible.

This is an ambitious task both over 42.195 kilometers and in the stairwell and requires an excellent body feeling and restraint in the first half of the race. Those who manage a negative split (i.e., running the second half of the race minimally faster than the first half) have a great chance of having optimally implemented their abilities.

Example: Donauturm Run-Up in Vienna

The Donauturm tower run in Vienna was THE stair run in Europe for two decades. In some years there was an intermediate time classification at the halfway point of the race, for which there was prize money of 300, 200 and 100 euros.

The Pole Tomasz Klinz had it in for this prize and proved how hard and long the race can be if you run on reserve from the halfway point, because while he was in the lead at the halfway point with 1:39 minutes and I was in third place with 1:47 minutes, the positions rotated in the second half.

4.12 Study on Tactics for Stair Running

In 2008 and 2009, the University of Milan conducted a study on stair running in the Italian capital to find out which tactic is the most successful in tower running. As one of the very first scientific studies in tower running, Minetti et al. (2009) came to the following conclusion, among others:

A more in-depth analysis seems to indicate that the best runners (i.e., those with a higher-than-average vertical speed) show a more uniform ascent profile, without an inflection point (figure 6). Also, an early inflection point seems to be negatively related to the overall performance. Only one athlete decided to change his profile in the second half of the ascent by increasing his velocity. He saved some energy for the last part of the race, but he did not win despite having increased the average vertical speed, underlining our hypothesis that best performance is associated with a uniform ascent profile (figure. 7).

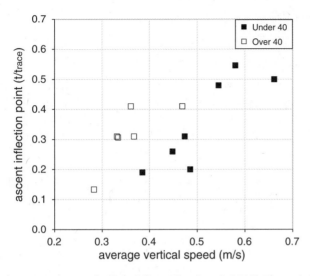

Figure 1 Average vertical speed (from Minetti et al., 2009). The study is available at: https://minetti2009.thomasdold.com.

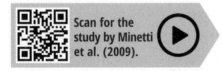

Scan for the study by Minetti et al. (2009).

4.13 Supportive Strength Exercises

In terms of muscular strain, running stairs is a special kind of exertion that can be just as conditional as road running, mountain running, or running in sports.

The energy supply—the total load on the cardiovascular system and on individual muscle groups—is different. Anyone who has run 100, 200, or even 1,000 steps at a stretch knows this.

In order to better cope with the muscular strain, there are special strengthening exercises. That's why you'll find chapters that include exercises for strengthening, coordination and stretching in this book. There are also general strengthening exercises without stairs that support training on stairs.

Lateral torso muscles ★

Starting position:

Sit on the floor and raise your upper body and legs. Keep your gaze on your toes. Make sure that both your back and legs are straight; the exercise will be easier if you bend your knees.

Exercise description:

Turn your upper body to the left side and your legs to the right side and vice versa. In this way you train the shear forces that occur when changing direction and the resulting centrifugal forces on the landings.

Reps: 6–12 times per side

Rest: One minute between sets

Sets: 2–4 times

Strong training effect: Lateral abdominal muscles

VARIATION:

Hold a heavy medicine ball with both hands and touch the floor to the right and left of your hips. If you want to use a towel, a water bottle, or a shoe, these will work too.

Squats

One of the classics to train the front thigh muscles.

Starting position:

Stand with your legs hip-width apart and straighten your upper body.

Exercise description:

Now bring your buttocks back and down as if you were sitting down. Keep your knees behind an imaginary vertical line above the toes of your feet; the shins are almost vertical. In addition, keep your back and spine straight. For most people, a straight back feels like they have a hollow back.

Important tips:

1. Hold a stick behind your neck above your shoulder blades with both hands. Elbows are bent 90 degrees. It's easier to keep your back straight when you go down because your hands can't fall forward. With practice, you won't need this support.

2. Place a four-inch thick book or something similar, such as a weight plate or a piece of wood, under your heel. This will ensure that even if you have shortened Achilles tendons, the body load will remain primarily on your heels during the exercise.

3. Perform this exercise with only the stick (i.e., without weights) at the beginning. You will then use your own body weight to train tendons, ligaments, and cartilage for higher loads and learn the technique more easily. Good technique is extremely important in this strengthening exercise.

TRAINING ZONES

The body provides energy through various sources. The provision and training of each is not just a theoretical science, but requires different practical adaptations from body to body. Training that works for one athlete may not work in the same way for another. Even the same training works differently for the same athlete because of the constant adaptation to each new session. As a result, the path to peak performance is very individual. Therefore, top athletes have their own coaches and training plans, which are continuously created and adapted for them.

The generally valid basics of running are explained in this chapter from the perspective of stair running. In addition, the focus is on the special features that must be observed in staircase running training, since it cannot be compared with any other training and has its own laws.

5.1 Health Check and Performance Test

Before you start with the intensive stair training, a health check and a spiroergometry are highly recommended. In addition to information about the health of your heart (e.g., blood pressure, ECG), you will also receive an assessment of your body's ability to withstand stress and its maximum capacity.

The measurement of the reactions of the heart, circulation, respiration, and metabolism under stress also enables retrospective conclusions to be drawn about the metabolic situation and allows statements to be made about the quality of the training.

Spiroergometric (lactate) performance diagnostics therefore serve to record the actual state of health and enable sensible progress monitoring and training control, in addition to the good feeling and the knowledge that you are healthy!

Looking at the training range from the maximum heart rate makes the most sense for stair running. There are also models that are based on maximum performance (in competition) or on the target finishing time (e.g., in a marathon). These training models work directly with running speeds. The unit of measurement is then not the pulse, but minutes per kilometer/mile.

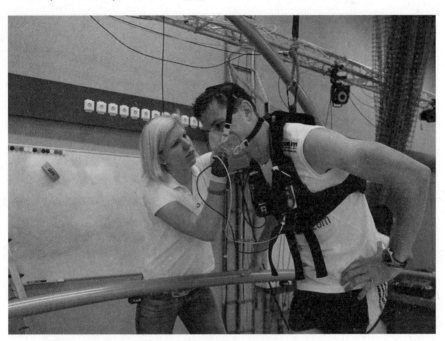

Spiroergometry with simultaneous lactate test to determine training status.

5.2 Training Zone: Regeneration or Recom (= light gray in the graphic)

The regeneration zone (zone 2 in the five-zone model) is below 65 percent of the maximum heart rate (HR_{max}) and is the lowest load zone. It is primarily used for active recovery after intense workouts. Many athletes find it difficult to run slowly because they do not believe in the training effect and therefore run too fast. This lightest form of running is ideal for the warm-up and cool-down of a training session, as a recovery run the day after a hard workout or competition, or for breaks between interval sessions. The low intensity allows for maximum blood flow to the muscles and thus encourages faster recovery. Recovery is more effective than at absolute rest because more blood is circulating.

The most important adaptation processes in the regeneration zone are:

- active support of the regeneration and adaptation processes in the body;
- warming up and blood circulation of the muscles;
- improvement of fat metabolism; and
psychological recovery.

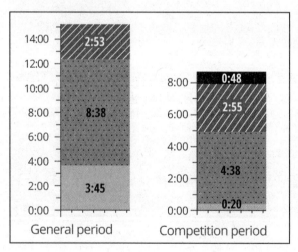

Figure 2 Comparison of training zones and times.

5.3 Basic Endurance 1 (= dotted area in the graphic)

The pulse is between 65–80 percent of the maximum heart rate (HRmax). The GA-1 zone is used to develop the performance base and builds the foundation for the performance development and the intensive stair training sessions. The GA-1 zone is the main part of the workout, accounting for about 70 percent of the total endurance workout, and the pace is low and easy to maintain.

Nevertheless, the body is challenged. Afterwards, it needs regeneration to carry out the adaptation processes. The proportion of fat burning in the energy supply is particularly large in GA-1 training; it is therefore referred to as fat metabolism training.

The rule of thumb is that runners can still talk well while running; you can tell long stories with a running buddy or in self-talk. Most importantly, long endurance runs or bike training are done in the GA-1 range. This training forms the foundation for the high-intensity sessions in stair running. The broader your foundation in the GA-1 range, the more stable the peak will be.

The most important adaptive processes in the GA-1 range are:

- Development and stabilization of basic endurance (i.e., the foundation of your athletic performance);

- Improvement of the regeneration ability;

- Improved blood flow to the muscles and supply of nutrients due to the *capillarization* (capillaries = finest of the blood vessels; capillarization involves the opening of dormant capillaries, the lengthening or widening of existing capillaries, or the formation of new ones);

- Enlargement and multiplication of mitochondria (mitochondria produce energy in the form of adenosine triphosphate (ATP) via the respiratory chain);

- Improved oxygen uptake, storage, and processing in the muscles;

- Improved oxygen uptake by the heart;

- Reduction of resting and exercise pulse (resting pulse of a non-athlete: 60–90 beats/minute; resting pulse of an endurance athlete: 30–50 beats/minute);

- Economization of the heart (i.e., the same or improved performance at a lower heart rate).

5.4 The Black Hole of Training

When transitioning between zones GA 1 and GA 2, your energy production is in the aerobic–anaerobic transition or mixed zone. Frequent training in this range usually leads to stagnation in performance development. This training range is called the black hole of training because the desired results do not occur; instead, your energy and effort in training disappears in a black hole. Athletes who frequently train in the black hole are training both too hard and not hard enough.

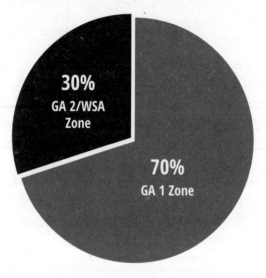

EXPERT TIP

Endurance training should consist of a mixture of different types of training in a ratio of 70:30. Seventy percent of the training time should be spent in the fat metabolism training zone (GA-1 zone) and only 30 percent of the training time should be spent in the GA-2 and WSA zone.

5.5 Basic Endurance 2 (GA 2 = striped in the graphic)

To become more efficient, you need the GA-2 training zone, where the heart rate is between 85–95 percent of the HRmax. In this range, you can exchange words and short instructions with your running partner. There is no air for sentences or stories. Energy is provided mainly through carbohydrate metabolism during this workout. Due to the high performance, the muscles consume more carbohydrates in addition to fats, because these can be metabolized with less oxygen and provide higher energy rates. In this power range, it becomes difficult to exchange complete sentences with your running partner. You focus more on yourself, your breathing, and best of all, your running technique. This workout is designed to increase performance.

The GA-2 range supports the following adaptations:

- Performance improvement;

- Improvement of VO2max (= maximum amount of oxygen that can be processed by the body during maximum effort);

- Development of performance in the aerobic–anaerobic zone;

- Heart volume increase;

- Increase of lactate tolerance in muscle and body;

- Increase of the load tolerance in high pulse ranges; and

- Economization of the running technique.

5.6 Competition-Specific Endurance/Anerobic
(= black in the graphic)

The heart rate in this range is more than 95 percent of the HRmax. Talking is no longer possible due to the maximum load. Your attention is on running technique and breathing. In addition to burning fats and carbohydrates with oxygen, the body now also uses oxidative processes without oxygen.

In the oxidative energy supply without oxygen (anaerobic), there are degradation products (lactate) that build up faster in this load range than they can be degraded at the same time. The lactate accumulates in the bloodstream and in the body, which is why muscles hurt. After a certain period of time, the lactate forces the athlete to stop the training or competition or to reduce the performance/speed. Your body needs a lot of recovery from this high-intensity training, which can take up to 48 hours for the body and 72 hours for the central nervous system. Extensive GA-1 training has a positive impact on these recovery times.

The WSA training supports the following adaptations:

- Performance improvement;

- Increasing exercise tolerance in the anaerobic range;

- Will training;

- Strengthening of tendons and muscles at maximum load; and

- Preparing the body and mind for a high-intensity competitive load.

There is extensive, in-depth literature and studies on the training zones and performance improvement topics. In addition, many studies change and what was current 10 years ago is now partly discussed scientifically in the opposite direction.

My recommendation: The practical test

Test for yourself how well you feel when you implement them. If it feels strange, inappropriate, or wrong, you can read other books and studies and then use them to check if the theory fits better in the practice test. Everybody is individual and you will experience this during training as well. If you follow the basic laws of the following chapters, there is no right or wrong training, only training that serves and does not serve your goal.

6 TRAINING METHODS

The body is trained most effectively with training methods tailored to the training goal, performance level, experience, and training terrain.

Only running the same distance at the same pace is the worst case for performance development from the point of view of sports science. The monotonous stimuli cause no or very little adaptation processes. Therefore, in this chapter you will find the possible training methods and their specific use for stair running.

6.1 Continuous Method

You build the foundation of your training and physical performance with the continuous method and the steady-state run as the corresponding training unit.

The constant load improves your basic endurance and allows you to recover quickly even after high-intensity sessions. In very endurance-oriented disciplines, such as marathons, the endurance run can last several hours. For stair running it is shorter. Between 30 and 100 minutes are sufficient to build the foundation for short stair runs with loads between two and 30 minutes.

EXPERT TIP

If you want to train longer and more often, you can switch to a bike for this training method. Low- to moderate-intensity cycling is easier on the joints than running. In addition, the motion of cycling is similar to climbing stairs as you train to put your foot on the stairs from above and push yourself up. The cadence should be between 80 and 95 rpm to allow for fluid and powerful pedaling and movement.

The continuous method optimizes fat metabolism at low load. Therefore, with practice, you can exercise for several hours without energy supply. In the basic periods, many weeks or months before the competition, training with the continuous method in low pulse ranges makes sense. Later, higher load and pulse ranges are added. In this way, you expand your load tolerance, including the training of fat and carbohydrate burning.

6.2 Intensive and Extensive Continuous Method

In addition to the normal continuous method, there are two special forms:

In the **intensive endurance method**, the load is higher (e.g., because you run faster than in the endurance method). This means that more carbohydrates are needed and their metabolism is trained.

In the **extensive endurance method**, you try to extend the duration of the load and thus train the body's efficient use of energy reserves. In addition, you put an intense stimulus on the muscles throughout the long duration, which triggers an adaptation effect.

6.3 Fartlek

The fartlek method is a form of training with changes of pace, which can last from a few seconds to several minutes, depending on the training. As a rule, the sessions include frequent changes of pace in different sections and you train without recovery breaks.

The variation in training is very well suited to bring variety into the running training, especially as a contrast to the continuous method.

Example: Kenyan Fartlek

This is a standard program for many runners, especially in marathons, to prepare for the big races.

Ten to twenty minutes of warm-up is followed by 10–20 blocks of 30 seconds of exertion; the break, in which the runners continue at a slightly reduced speed, also lasts 30 seconds. This is immediately followed by 10–20 times of 60 seconds of exertion, again with the same amount of rest at a slightly slower speed. After 10–20 minutes of cool-down, the session (and usually the runner) is done.

Those who train this session and run at high or higher speeds during the load periods will feel both the accumulative stress and the training effect after some time. These units create improvements in energy supply and load tolerance. In the intensive form, the load can extend into the competition-specific range (WSA). In the extensive form, training takes place with more or longer intervals, if necessary, primarily in the GA-1 range but also in the GA-2 range.

The training location of the world champions and Olympic champions: Kamariny Running track in Iten, Kenya.

6.4 Interval Method

With the alternation of load and recovery phases in a training session, the load accumulates. In the recovery phases you regenerate—usually only partially. There are many concepts as to when the recovery phase is sufficient (e.g., a rewarding break is when the pulse falls below 120 beats per minute), but this does not take into account how well the musculature and mental willpower are restored.

The Extensive Interval Method

- The extensive interval method is used to develop strength and basic endurance capacity.

- Athlete has a medium load intensity in the aerobic-anaerobic metabolic range.

- The lactate is 3–6 millimoles per liter.

- The duration of the session is 30–180 minutes.

- The interval break is 1–3 minutes.

- During the recovery phases, the heart rate drops by more than 20 beats per minute.

EXPERT TIP

With the extensive interval method you can see how good your base endurance is. During the breaks, your heart rate drops faster and more. If you have more base endurance, your recovery ability is higher. Athletes with good base endurance can recover faster and stronger in the intervals and thus train more and possibly faster intervals.

In staircase training how fast you can recover from a high-intensity interval to train another interval is of central importance.

The Intensive Interval Method

The intensive interval method consists of several successive interval loads of 15-60 seconds length, demands a high intensity, and has an interval break of 15-90 seconds.

The muscular load increases with the number of intervals; lactate concentration is poorly reduced during the short intervals, and the training of motor requirements close to competition and their stabilization takes place. An increase in anaerobic performance is achieved and the maximum oxygen uptake (VO2max) improves.

Insight Into Professional Training

During the writing of this book, I had so much desire for stair running that I went to Frankfurt. In the MAINTOWER, I have been able to complete hundreds of training sessions since 2005 through an exemption.

This workout, or the pulse and elevation curve, exemplifies how the load and heart rate increases when running up.

Within the first minute, the pulse rate shoots up and then rises more slowly. During the 185 meters of altitude, there were two pauses of about one minute each, resulting in a drop in heart rate. In addition, it can be seen that the heart rate increases from the first to the second ascent, both during the session and at the end of the breaks. The reduction of the heart rate decreases; the recovery is not as fast.

You can probably easily imagine that the body copes with 185 meters of altitude and 52 floors a little worse the second time; this is exactly what these curves and numbers visualize.

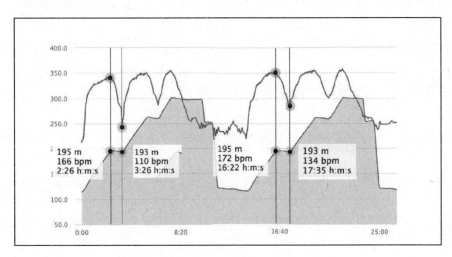

Figure 3 Training session MAINTOWER summer 2022.

6.5 Repetition Method

The loads are short and high intensity, there are high lactate concentrations measured during the first load phase. There is a complete recovery during the breaks—active/passive breaks of 30 minutes or longer to regenerate the body functions. Two to eight repetitions are performed. The characteristics of the competition load are developed by training the anaerobic-aerobic metabolism, and the heart volume develops.

Insight Into Professional Training

The repetition method is high intensity and is suitable for stair training to create a competition-like situation shortly before an actual competition. The body can respond to this maximum stimulus with an adaptation and the stair climber can benefit from this on race day. It should be noted that stair running is ALWAYS very demanding and stressful on the body and mind.

With the repetition method, it is very easy to bring the body and mind into a state of overtraining. Therefore, this training method is only suitable for experienced competitive athletes and should only be used very selectively.

I usually trained only a mixed form of the competition and interval methods before the major international races. The recovery was physically and mentally faster and easier than in training sessions with pure repetition methods.

6.6 Competition Method

This method leads to the development and testing of the endurance ability specific to the competition. The load corresponds to the competition load (e.g., through competition tests and performance control tests), and is based on the requirements of the main competition.

Pro Experience

Nothing is as exhausting as running stairs, even after several years of training. No road run, track race, mountain run, or marathon can put the same strain on the body as a stair run. It feels like an 800-meter run that lasts 3–12 minutes.

Running stairs at full speed, with all muscles and all power engaged.

Therefore, especially after a few months of concentration on training, the preparation for the main competition is essential. For this purpose, I like to use another stair run to bring the body to the absolute limits and to shift them.

I like to picture a not-quite-clean water pipe flushed with high pressure during a competition; then the capillaries, the airways, and all other functions in the body are opened to the maximum. Whether or not this picture corresponds with reality, the results speak for themselves.

If no other competition is possible, I run the 52 floors in the MAINTOWER without a break at maximum speed. The mental attitude is key. Alone in the stairwell, I can feel how intense this load is in my entire body.

Through frequent mental training, the body and mind can get into the mood for competition without a starting gun, official timing, or opponents, and can perform such feats in the solitude of the training stairwell.

This is not suitable for everyone, but it brings many advantages and opportunities. Chapter 19 contains many tips on this.

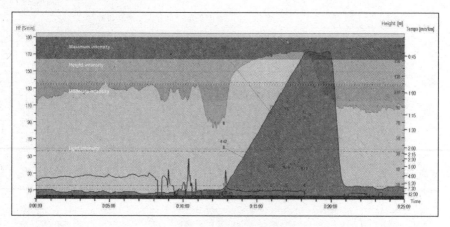

Figure 4 Pulse curve of a training session according to the competition method: warm-up, once up and down the MAINTOWER at full speed, cool-down.

Done after over 1,000 steps!

7 TRAINING PLANNING AND CONTROL

A training plan describes all the actions and measures an athlete uses to reach a specific training goal within a defined span of time.

There are also many planning and control models in other areas (e.g., in economics). In the economic sector, similar models can be used, which are exemplary for sports training planning. The model of the **control loop** demonstrates the individual steps of the training in the ideal case.

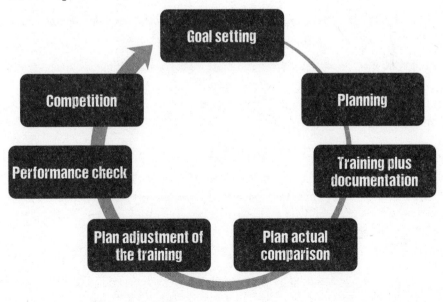

Figure 5 Planning and control in sports.

7.1 Goal Setting: What Do You Want?

What's your goal? Finishing or a record time?

This is the first and most important question in elite sports and at the same time the first and most important question in sports in general.

As individual as people and athletes are, so too are the goals, possibilities, and resources that someone has available. Clear statements like: "I want to finish a marathon in 2:59:59 hours" are much more difficult to make in stair running, because the competition time can only be roughly estimated.

Time Goal

Every tower and every staircase is different and therefore you can only roughly estimate a realistic finishing time from the number of steps, meters in height, and floors.

Placement Goal

"I want to be first!" Or is it the other way around and you don't want to be last?

Winning is one way of setting goals, especially if you are dominating a sport like Eliud Kipchoge, Roger Federer, or Michael Schumacher.

Or is it the other way around—you don't want to be last?

Both extremes, statistically speaking, apply to very few runners. With all placement goals, it is also important to consider, in contrast to the individual time goals, who also starts or does not start. Thus these goals are often a little vague (e.g., finish in the first third of competitors, finish in the midfield). Therefore, setting goals via external parameters in staircase running, such as time and placement, is rather difficult and unsatisfactory.

It will be easier for you if you participate in a tower run several times. Then you can measure yourself. In a modified way this even works for the first time you run a tower:

- How do I want to feel when I reach the finish line?

- In which attitude do I want to run the stairs?

- Should I go all out or save energy for sightseeing afterwards?

These questions should not only be asked for a competition, but for every training session.

- What is my goal?

- How intensively do I want to work outside my comfort zone?

- How much time do I have?

- What other (training) loads do I have to plan for (e.g., if running stairs serve as a supplement)?

A good coach will help you clearly articulate your goals. It may also be that you realize that you like to have vague goals (i.e., to have no measurability). This is also a form of clarity that is valuable for training planning.

7.2 Planning

In many sports, planning for an upcoming competition, with appropriate basic, advanced, and peak training, begins several years in advance. There is a systematic approach with a foundation that is built like a pyramid.

Keep in mind that one year of basic training in the GA-1 zone is not followed by a year in the GA-2 zone, and so on. Instead, in each year, everything is trained, but in different weighting. In the first year of the multi-year plan, lower load ranges are trained with high volumes. In the last year, the volume in the lower range will no longer increase, but the focus will be on high-intensity competition-specific training.

This very superficial strategic view in the multi-year planning breaks down into annual plans and these result in several **macro plans** that control the training over several months.

The next step in the top-down planning are the **microcycles**, which represent the respective training weeks. The last link in the planning chain is the individual training units, ensuring that each individual training unit is derived from the BIG goal. Conversely, each training unit serves the BIG goal.

Besides this theoretical point of view, you will notice that planning is one thing, the framework, the direction, the fixed star. However, as illustrated at the beginning of the chapter, it needs training adjustments, sometimes even daily, because the athlete and the body do not function according to the plan. Otherwise, it would not be so complex to perform at the highest level, nor would it be anything special. The fact that you need fine-tuning and readjustment in everyday training is what makes a trainer relevant.

It's a reminder that even with the best plan, you can't have everything under control. Even with the best and most successful people in the world, there is luck and chance. And yes, the proportion is getting smaller and smaller among the best of the best. Seen from the outside, they function like Swiss clockwork. But that is an illusion.

7.2.1 Single Events

Long-term planning becomes more difficult for important individual events without a multi-year goal: "I want to run a marathon once in my life" could be an example of this. In tower running, it is necessary to prepare for two or three competitions within a few days/weeks and then start a new cycle.

The cycles can only build on each other to a limited extent in terms of training methods, because an absolute highlight takes place in each competition block, which demands full focus and maximum performance. The preparations last between two and six months and include a phase of basic training, a phase of build-up training, and then specific training on the stairs. The individual areas merge into one another and are not seen as separate sections, but rather as training priorities in this section.

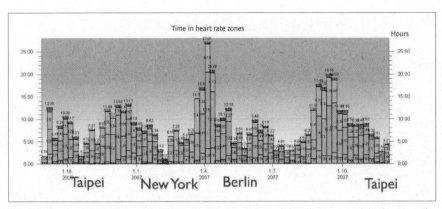

Figure 6 Exemplary multi-year planning with the respective training time per week in the respective pulse ranges including competition highlights (2006–2007).

Figure:

This is what training looked like in 2006 and 2007. In addition to the competition locations of the respective highlights in the period, the months/years are entered on the lower axis.

The height of the bars indicates the training time per week in hours. Strength training with the body or on equipment as well as stretching must be added to the indicated training time.

The peak in spring and fall is due to long bike rides in general endurance zone. These are not so long in winter, because they were rather more intensive on the ergometer indoors.

7.3 Training and Documentation

The data recording takes place during daily training with a heart rate monitor (chest strap or on the wrist). The heart rate, speed (via GPS), and most other parameters such as altitude, temperature, and stride length are displayed and recorded. In addition, the runner can collect further training and performance data using various methods.

CK Value Measurement

This value indicates the degree of muscle damage (e.g., due to intensive training). The value increases with increased muscular load and is associated with muscle soreness at high values.

Lactate Measurement

This measures the accumulation of the breakdown products of lactic acid. When normal energy production with oxygen (aerobic) is insufficient to meet energy needs, glucose is metabolized to produce energy. This is followed without oxygen (anaerobic) to form lactate. In order to break down lactate, it must be converted into carbon dioxide and water.

This means that lactate levels rise during high exertion levels in training or competition, because the breakdown of lactic acid in the heart muscle is slower than its formation during very high exertion levels. The range in which just as much lactate is built up and broken down is called the **steady state** or **threshold**. This is where training changes from predominantly aerobic to predominantly anaerobic.

Spiroergometry

In addition to an ECG for cardiac activity, the air is also measured with regard to its composition of oxygen O_2 and carbon dioxide CO_2. Based on these parameters, conclusions can be drawn as to how much oxygen the body metabolizes and from this the aerobic performance is determined.

This selection of procedures and measurement methods can be used in both field and ergometer training. For some years now, mobile spiroergometer devices have been available that athletes can wear during training.

The measurement procedures are complex and disturbing for a regular, relaxed training routine. For this reason, these methods are used in special test training sessions, often under standardized conditions (e.g., on a treadmill or a cycle ergometer), and according to a standardized protocol in order to make the values comparable.

For stair running, for example, the parameters provide information about basic endurance, lactate threshold, and the pulse and speed ranges of the training. A termination test can also show how high the lactate tolerance and the load resistance are. The speed is increased until the athlete stops the test due to overload.

In all tests, it should be noted that stair running is very specific and cannot be compared to cycling and running on a treadmill. Even a stair treadmill, which moves steps in a similar way to an escalator, cannot imitate stair running. The rest of the uncertainty, even when using all the testing procedures, must be balanced with body awareness and experience.

7.4 Plan: Actual Comparison of Training

With the training plan and the recorded data, the training analysis shows the variations.

If you train at the maximum performance level, you will be confronted with variations. These can result from external influences or from the athlete's body and mind. Even the best coaches with the most sophisticated training plans and scientific methods can never see into the athlete's body and mind. It remains a game in a black box. Target values are integrated, the athlete trains these, and then it is observed which performance capacity and which performance can be called up.

Exactly how performance is created—or not created—remains only partially measurable and observable. Therefore, the target–performance comparison looks at where differences have arisen between planning and result. This data forms the basis for training adjustments.

7.5 Plan Adjustment

It is best if the training plan is followed as planned and the results and findings are incorporated into the next microcycle planning. If the difference is large, an adjustment will help to keep the plan on target. The extent of this adaptation is based on experience and is very individual—like all training planning.

Pro Experience

With high-intensity loads, such as in stair running, there is an increased risk that physical performance will be overstimulated. It is possible that you will exceed a limit with some stair jumps or runs, at which you will need multiple days of recovery. For example, a 10 percent increase in effort will require 300 percent more recovery. For example, one more interval increases recovery from two days to one week. This is more likely to happen with trained athletes who have a very high-performance level. In normal performance ranges for non-professional athletes, massive effects are unusual. You need a lot of training and a very strong will to be able to train in these fragile, painful high-performance zones.

7.6 Success Control

The success control can take place in a test in the laboratory or in a competition. It becomes clear whether the planning and implementation are successful. It shows whether the plan for the athlete leads to his goal achievement or must be adapted.

How nice it is when you have implemented a plan and in the end the result is achieved as desired. This is the dream of many athletes and even more trainers, but sports and competitions show that in reality things work differently, and athletes who consistently achieve success are rare.

7.7 Planning or Instinct?

In addition to the more or less precise planning of training, there are athletes who train by instinct. Whether top runners from Africa or Europe, there are athletes everywhere who do not follow any training schedule. A connection between the level of performance and the intensity of training control is usually obvious. For inexperienced, young athletes it is also difficult to reach their maximum performance level without training control, because the knowledge and experience regarding training methodology is missing. Therefore, it is advisable to start with a training plan. With the experience gained, after a few months or years you can consider what you want to adjust on your own. Many athletes also love training plans because the decision of what to train today is taken away.

Another psychological point is the self-fulfilling prophecy. It is psychologically more likely that you will reach your goal if you have a path or plan to get there. For example, a treasure map is not necessary for finding treasure, but with the map it will be much easier and probably faster to find.

If the training is not intended to reach a goal, the question of the necessity of training control is different. Experience shows that every runner has a goal, even if best times and performance are unimportant. There are many other individual goals. Regardless of what your goal is, it is worthwhile to know it very clearly and to consider what your path to the goal looks like and what mindset you have for it. The planning and control process can be useful for this in an adapted form.

8 THREE TIMES UP AND DOWN MAINTOWER FOR WORLDWIDE SUCCESS

There is actually no typical training for a competitive athlete, as the body responds best to new stimuli. In the stairwell, I train for a very specific load—running 200-300 meters ascent or more at maximum speed. For this you need a variety of training, a lot of basic training, and specific training on the stairs.

Even if the training is very varied, there are certain sessions that you can take as a benchmark, that you like to train and that repeat themselves, more or less often. The stair session that makes my heart beat faster, physically and emotionally, is running up the 1,090 steps, 190 meters of altitude, and 52 floors of the MAINTOWER in Frankfurt three times. This is my session, which I love and respect at the same time.

It is what stair running is, to be absolutely honest. There is no bad weather and there are no excuses because the only parameters that change in the stairwell are my own responsibility—physically and mentally. This session is how I have prepared for all my tower running victories. With the split and finish times, I can tell exactly how fit my body is today, how big the improvement is, and where I can develop in the coming days and weeks. It shows me where the deficits are and which pulse ranges I need to train more or less. This session demands everything from me, and in doing so, it exposes everything and makes connections transparent—for me.

I rarely share the stair moments with others. Sometimes employees from the local state bank or the law firms pass by for a few floors in the emergency stairwell, while I run up, sweating and panting. These are brief encounters in a flyby for a moment.

It took a long time to get the special permit for this particular stairwell. But since Christmas 2005, there is hardly anyone who has run the stairs in the MAINTOWER more often and faster. We share a very special relationship and love.

Due to many other factors, such as studies, work, and the urge for efficiency, the sessions are timed to the maximum and are completed from start to finish at breakneck speed.

1. Arrival at Frankfurt Main main station.

2. The exit is as far forward as possible in the ICE, in order to get quickly into the S-Bahn station.

3. Down the escalator or normal steps? It doesn't matter; the main thing is to get there fast.

4. Take the S-Bahn to the Taunusanlage and already be mentally in the stairwell.

5. Register at the back entrance, get the key, and go into the building.

6. Change clothes.

7. Get out of the tower and warm up a run (1–2 kilometers) in the park of the Taunusanlage.

8. Back to the tower and get body and mind ready with coordination exercises.

9. Five minutes of gentle stretching/mobilization.

10. Let security know I'm ready and go straight to the stairwell in summer or take off the long warm-up clothes beforehand in winter.

11. The lock is unlocked, the door is open, and after a "Have fun" from the security person, I am alone with the stairs in the stairwell.

12. Take a breath and prepare the watch.

13. GOOO!!!!

14. 1,090 steps/52 floors.

15. Made it! Rest 20–30 seconds on the last step, then through the building to the elevator.

16. Push the button, wait, breathe, and travel back down in the visitor elevator.

17. Through the catacombs back to security and then together again to the stairwell door.

18. Take a five-minute break to calm the pulse.

19. GOOO!!!!

20. 1,090 steps/52 floors including a 60-second break on floor 30.

21. Done! Rest 20–30 seconds on the last step, then through the building to the elevator.

22. Press the button, wait, breathe, and travel back down in the visitor elevator.

23. Through the catacombs back to security, then back together to the stairwell door.

24. A five-minute break in total.

25. 1,090 steps/52 floors with a 60-second break on floors 20 and 40.

26. Made it! One-minute breath on the last step, then through the building to the elevator.

27. Press the button, wait, breathe, and travel back down in the visitor elevator.

28. Walk through the catacombs back to security.

29. Head out to the Taunusanlage for a 1 kilometer cool-down.

30. Return to the tower.

31. Wash body and change clothes.

32. Go back to the S-Bahn—running, if I'm late.

33. From the S-Bahn sometimes via the escalator, often via the normal steps to the platform.

34. Wait a few minutes or walk along the ICE as long as possible.

35. Board.

36. Post-process in the train with stretching, eating, drinking, and evaluating training data.

This sequence is so well-rehearsed that it runs like Swiss clockwork in 1:50–2:10 hours. The training in Frankfurt runs just as precisely as the worldwide victories. This precision, no excuses, unconditional performance, and almost no breaks even at maximum load are the behaviors that I improve in training. These are the basics, besides physical strength, for many victories.

The question of "Why do you do this to yourself?" arises immediately for many people. For me as a runner, this training is excellent and the training opportunity in the MAINTOWER is ideal. These sessions are the backbone of my body's performance in the stair runs. In addition, other factors—and permission to run in the television tower in Stuttgart and in the Park Inn Hotel on Alexanderplatz in Berlin—have helped to prepare the legs and the body for the tower runs around the world.

In Frankfurt I am by far the most frequent and the people who make this possible also have a big share in the winner's trophies. It's easy to imagine how great it is to meet and be accompanied by people who like what you're doing, support you, and always have a funny joke.

Often the body, and sometimes the mind, are sour and all the people who support me are more help on the demanding staircase journey. Therefore, not only personally, but also at this point to all these supporters: THANK YOU!

Stair training in the Maintower as a basis for international competitions.

Interview: I'm Already There!

By Jürgen Löhle for the STUTTGARTER Zeitung

Thomas Dold from the Kinzigtal is one of the best stair runners in the world. And I am not one at all. An unequal race over the 52 floors, 1,090 steps, and 190 meters of altitude of the MAINTOWER in Frankfurt.

MAINTOWER Frankfurt, stairwell, seventh floor:

Thomas Dold hurries past, doesn't even look at me. Always two steps at a time, the railing on which he swings around the corners shakes. I'm shaking a bit, too, especially my thighs. I still have 45 floors to climb in a windowless stairwell that, thanks to the invention of elevators, is really only meant for emergencies. Or for people who just want to cover one or two floors without an elevator. Dold, on the other hand, still has a whopping 97 floors to go, plus an elevator ride down. And he wants to do the whole thing faster than I can do 45. Well, then.

Thomas Dold? That's right, the 28-year-old from Steinach in the Kinzig Valley, who can run up stairs like no one else in the world. The economics graduate began playing soccer as a youngster, and in 2001 he tried his hand at mountain running, which is an obvious sport in the Black Forest. He was a member of the national team until 2006, but three years earlier, in 2003, Dold specialized in exotic sports such as backward running and tower running.

He has 41 victories worldwide to his credit, and in 2008 he climbed the 2,046 steps with a height difference of 390 meters in the **Taipei 101** skyscraper in 10:53 minutes. But he is best known for one thing: From 2006 to 2012, he won the race to the top of the *Empire State Building* in New York seven times in a row, running up 1,576 steps and climbing 320 meters to the viewing platform on the 86th floor. The prize for the winner after just over 10 minutes of slogging up the stairs? "A handshake," says Dold, for whom New York is important.

This is where the names of the scene are made, the race in New York's landmark is the most popular run-up in the world. This February, Thomas Dold had to cancel the race in the Big Apple due to flu. The next goal could now be the 2,041 steps in the *World Summit Wing Hotel* in Beijing. The next big tower run will take place there on August 3. Possibly with him, negotiations are still underway.

I see Dold's back for a few seconds, then he's gone, disappeared on his way up. I hear his breathing for a while longer, then it's quiet again. The staircase in the main building of the Hessische Landesbank covers a height of about 190 meters up to the 52nd floor. White walls, mousy gray steps, stainless steel railings, a change of direction every nine steps. The whole thing is mostly windowless, fully air-conditioned and about as cozy as a hamster wheel.

Actually, we were supposed to do a normal portrait story, but Thomas Dold had the idea of letting the reporter experience what it feels like to race upwards. We'll start running together, that's his plan, and he'll try to outrun me. I "only" have 1,090 steps to climb, he 2,180—and an elevator ride down. On the phone, I spontaneously said yes, and now I'm on the 11th floor and thinking of Dold's question an hour ago when we met in Mannheim on the ICE. "Your pump is already okay, right?" I sincerely hope so, because my thighs are already burning, my breathing is rattling, and my pulse is hammering in my throat. Forty-one floors to go.

Thomas Dold was not always a tower runner. In his native southern Baden, he ran up the mountains of the Black Forest and was a member of the national team. The man likes to seek the thrill, the excitement of the unusual. That's why he's also a two-time world champion in backward running, but his greatest fascination comes from the stairs. Step after step at the limit, that appeals to his nature. The man likes to find his limits.

"The stairs are the steepest mountain," says Dold. And then he enthuses about the feeling of flying to the top, so to speak. Dold claims that running in joyless stairwells can also be a bit easy. An assessment that is difficult to understand, but good.

In New York, Dold's running talent and lightness have been tormenting not only himself since 2006, but above all the competition, which he regularly leaves behind him on the 1,576 steps. "You need passion for the sport," he says with a blissful smile on his face. But the emphasis is clearly on suffering. How? And what about easy?

Dold explains that you can run stairs casually as well as competitively— if you have the form for it. What he means by that, I felt on the way from the main station to MAINTOWER. Of course, the athlete ignored the escalator that leads up from the depths of the S-Bahn. I don't really have the passion for it, but the escalator is too slow to follow Dold and I don't know the way to the tower.

On the other hand, I understand the suffering well, very well. Twenty-fourth floor. Dold is probably almost at the top for the first time, but I don't care. I have developed a rhythm that keeps me alive: inhale, step, exhale, step. And again and again. When Dold flies to the top, it's more like stomping. Suddenly, a woman with two folders under her arm enters the stairwell; according to her look, I probably look pretty strange, to say the least. The lactate is probably already leaking out of my ears.

The woman in the lawyer and bank tower has certainly not often seen a guy with a collapsed red head in sports gear. After all, Dold is the only one who is allowed to train in the non-public stairwell with a special permit. Until Easter, the man from Baden kept himself fit on the 700 steps in Stuttgart's television tower. When the tower was closed to visitors for fire safety reasons, that was the end for him, too.

Now he has found asylum in the banking metropolis. By the way, I don't care if Dold laps me. But it's going to be hard for him, because I was complaining for so long before the start of our train ride (twice my age, the shape of a shoebox, knee problems) that Dold generously gave me the first seven floors in addition. "You can run in there in peace," he said. Seven floors to run—that sounds almost like a mockery to someone who appreciates escalators and elevators.

Running stairs also has something to do with structure. Stairs are a clearly defined thing, and Dold is a guy who likes that because he wants to use his time as effectively as possible. Running stairs is short, but intense. "You get to the finish faster than when you run uphill, so the pain is shorter but much more intense," he says.

Thomas Dold, who describes himself as an impulse generator, passes on his knowledge as a speaker at seminars, as a trainer, motivator, and team manager; he has also founded the association RUN2SKY.com e.V., under whose umbrella track and field athletes whose goal is to participate in the Olympic Games are to gather and whom Dold wants to support, especially in terms of mental training and running technique.

And what drives him to the stairwells of this world? "It's fascinating to test your psychological and physical limits," he says, and adds with a laugh: "Besides, there's no such thing as bad weather in stairwells."

That's true about the weather, but it doesn't help much now. Forty-fourth floor. My thighs are about to burst, or my coronary arteries, or both. There is a feeling called runner's high that describes the painless euphoria of physical exertion.

Nice for those who may experience it. I wait in vain. Forty-eighth floor, the sweat burns in my eyes, I have switched off the heart rate monitor. And suddenly there it is, the 52nd floor—and Dold is not there. He arrives 40 seconds later.

Shortly after, we're both sitting on the last step in front of the observation deck and we're breathing a sigh of relief. Of course, without the seven-story lead, I would have lost. But no matter, I feel like a winner because I have increased my personal best from 74 steps (underground parking to the third floor) to 1,090. And after a minute, I am flush with a fascination of the sport. Really nice when the pain eases.

But that can't be the only reason for this kind of sport. Dold also wants to show how important fitness is. In Stuttgart, he recently spent a day running up the 72 steps of the Stadtmitte S-Bahn station on behalf of a health insurance company against anyone who wanted to. He ran on the normal stairs, his opponents on the escalator, and only lost to one of them. "Everyone should have their little sporting challenge every day," he says.

My challenge ends after just under 13 minutes with muscle twitching and the sublime feeling of having accomplished something perhaps pointless, but certainly not ordinary. As I leave MAINTOWER a little stiff in the hips, Thomas Dold rushes up for the third time. "Otherwise it's not worth the effort," he says. On the way from the S-Bahn to the Main station building, I use the normal stairs.

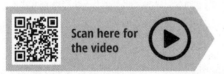

Scan here for the video ▶

Done! Thomas Dold and Jürgen Löhle high up on the MAINTOWER.

9 TYPICAL STAIR RUNNING SESSIONS

Maybe you're one of those lucky stair climbers who lives in a skyscraper and can climb stairs every day. There you have exceptional training opportunities—at least if you also have an exceptional physique. Then you can run and sprint many floors at a time without having to take a break.

For the beginning and up to a competitive level it is enough to train in a building with five floors. If you have more levels available, you can adapt the system and run more levels and floors at a time. If your building has only three floors, this is also suitable for the start. You will feel after a few sessions if you need change and adjustments.

Keep in mind that running stairs in a building with three or five floors will feel different than running stairs in a tower with 15, 25, or 50 floors.

As an analogy you can use a small pool, an Olympic pool, or the sea. You can swim in all three, but the feeling and the swimming will be different. That is, if you don't enjoy stair climbing in a very large building, it may be different in a small stairwell or on other stairs and vice versa.

A basic principle in stair training due to the high load is: ***More is not always better!***

You need the right balance between load and load tolerance. Start conservatively and see how your body reacts. For your first stair training session, take a number of floors that you are confident you can handle.

It is better for your performance development and for your body to increase the load than to have to drastically reduce the load in the next training after a session that was too intense. The load should go up like the staircase itself. This will keep you healthy and fit and increase your enjoyment of climbing stairs.

9.1 Where Do You Find Stairs?

Not everyone lives in a tall building or can take the stairs at work or at a friend's house. That doesn't matter, because there are many other options for your stair training.

9.1.1 Converting Floors to Outdoor Stairs

If you use an outdoor staircase, you can calculate one floor with 16 steps each. Thus, the outdoor staircase should have the equivalent of 80 steps for five floors. If you have 50 steps available, you can run more repetitions accordingly. However, more repetitions are not a must, because not only the number, but also the speed of your intervals determines the intensity. The same applies vice versa if your stairs have more than 100 steps.

9.1.2 Where Can You Train on the Stairs?

If you walk carefully through the cities and the countryside, you will be amazed at the number of opportunities for stair running. Everywhere there are differences in height to be overcome, whether at bridges, hills, buildings, parks, trains, or subways, there are stairs to be found. However, it is important to keep an eye on access restrictions, seasons, step characteristics, etc.

Parking garages/underground garages

This is often a very easy place to find stairs in cities. In addition to the stairs, the empty parking spaces can sometimes be used for additional exercise or recreation. In some parking garages there are even competitions. Many parking garages also have the advantage of no snow and ice in winter.

Training on parking decks and the stairs in the parking garage is varied.

Subway

Especially in wet weather, the underground staircases are a refuge for dry training. Away from the main paths, there are quieter staircases suitable for training on your own

A healthy day: staircase running campaign for more exercise.

A German health insurance company in Stuttgart had a very special idea. With the support of the escalator, everyone could compete against a professional stair runner. For one day, the Stadtmitte subway station became a place of very special movement, with the aim of creating more movement in everyday life.

Scan here for the video

Bridges

At the base of the bridges you can find stairs for your training. Most of them are large bridges over rivers, which need a high entrance on the shore, so that the boats can pass under the bridge in the middle. These structures on the shore are built with standardized steps of the same height, which are ideal for coordination exercises, jumps, and stretching. There are usually too few steps for running stairs.

Public buildings

Staircases are found in public buildings as elevated stairways or to connect floors. Whether at the town hall or at various offices and universities, there is a good chance of finding stairs for training. Sometimes it is better to inform the owners in advance so that nothing will stand in the way of the one-time or regular fun on the stairs.

Behind a church

In order to make large buildings flat, there may be height differences at the edges, where stairs are then built. Therefore, it is worthwhile to look around churches and large halls, where some steps may be waiting for you to train. These stairs are usually very little used and are therefore ideal for regular coordination, strengthening, and stretching exercises.

Between houses on the hillside

On the slopes of residential areas you can often find stairs. They connect the streets and are built with concrete or stone stairs. If you are lucky enough to have such stairs at your disposal, you can easily do an endurance run with stairs. To do this, you need to connect the stairs and the street to form a circuit on which you can run. Often these running tracks are illuminated, which is a real advantage for the dark season.

Vineyards

There are often stairs in the vineyards, which are usually accessible outside the time when the work on the vines takes place. The stairs are often challenging to walk because they have different angles of inclination. This is because the stairs adapt to the topography of the terrain. Unlike buildings, you are in the fresh air and in the middle of nature.

Mountain railroads

As an escape route, very long staircases are kept next to the track of mountain railroads. Built and maintained for emergencies, they often have a considerable length. The longest staircase of this type is located next to the Niesen mountain railroad in Switzerland. With 11,674 steps, it is the longest staircase in the world. Once a year, during the Niesen Stair Run, you can tackle this route and run all the way to the top of the 2,362-meter-tall mountain.

Hochfirst ski jump in Titisee-Neustadt, the largest natural ski jump in Germany.

Ski jump

The steep part of the hill where the jumpers are landing is ideal for practicing stair running. The steps at the edge of the jumping hill are often made of steel, so you have a flat step for your foot. At some jumps it is allowed and possible to run the steps next to the inrun tower all the way to the top. An advantage of the jump steps is that they have a flat tread and there is often a handrail to pull yourself up with your arms.

Europe Staircase in Partenen, Austria with over 4,000 steps and 700 meters of altitude.

9.1.3   Stäffele City Stuttgart

Perhaps not by chance, I lived and studied for several years in Stuttgart, the Stäffele city. It would be an exaggeration to say that I got fit for the international stair runs on the outside stairs. But built into the endurance runs, a few thousand more steps did the performance changer good. Anyone who lives in Stuttgart, or travels to the Swabian metropolis for business or pleasure, has the chance to participate in over 50 public relays that have their own name. There are a total of 600 Stäffele. At the same time, this raises the legitimate question: Why are there so many staircases in Stuttgart? The answer goes back a few hundred years, because at that time the people of Stuttgart farmed on the slopes. Since the 19th century, the population has increased and the slopes have been cultivated, the staircases integrated, and new ones built. The Willy Reichert staircase on the Karlshöhe is the longest Stäffele, with 408 steps.

9.1.4   DIN 18065 Regulates Stair Construction

According to the standard, the step length of an average person is 63 centimeters. These 63 centimeters are divided into two step heights and a step depth. This results in the standard of 18 centimeters step height (clearance dimension) and 27 centimeters step depth (tread). Thanks to German industrial standardization, we can walk steps quite automatically in Germany and also in many parts of Europe.

We have developed a habit that becomes especially apparent when it is broken. Very often, the clearance height in skyscrapers in other countries and continents is different, and therefore we need to be able to adapt quickly to the different step dimensions.

The optimal angle of inclination of a straight staircase is between 30 and 37 degrees. However, natural stairs have much steeper angles. The staircase next to the Niesen railroad has a maximum ascent of 67 degrees.

9.2 How Do You Incorporate Stair Running Into Running and Other Training Sessions?

40 Minutes of Continuous Running Plus 3 × 3 Flights of Stairs

After your endurance run, finish with the stairs, touching each step, using the 1-1 technique. The cadence is high so that the body gets a coordination and speed stimulus at the end of the session. This training method can be compared to acceleration runs at the end of an endurance run to maintain speed. It is essential for middle distance training and also for marathon training.

The difference between stair sprints and road sprints is that there is an increased coordination component and the stride length is predetermined by the steps. Another advantage, especially in winter, is that when it is wet or slippery outside, there is no danger of slipping on indoor steps.

Long Intervals (e.g., 4 × 1,000 meters including 5 × 30 steps)

The step runs serve to prepare the body and the autonomic nervous system for the actual training. This means that after the warm-up, you use the steps in the coordination part before the intervals, for example, in the stadium at the stands.

Run in the 1-1 technique and touch each step. Make sure your arms are swinging intensely and supporting you at a high frequency.

The number of intervals and distance is exemplary and also applies to other interval training sessions such as 8 × 800 meters.

Short Intervals for Sports
(e.g., 5 × 200 meters including 6 × 20 steps)   ★

Shorter interval runs are used to improve speed or speed endurance. With a distance of 200 meters, speed endurance is the training goal and after the warm-up you can activate speed with step runs.

Run up the steps at maximum frequency. The break is to run at least very slowly back the way you came. If you allow yourself a few extra seconds, the muscles and energy stores will recover more.

Pro Focus Tip

Stop at the bottom of the stairs for 20-30 seconds and focus on your next run, your breathing, and what you are looking for in your next run. Practical tests have shown that this focus immediately before an exercise or interval measurably improves the training result.

Sprints for Sports
(e.g., 5 × 80 meters including 4 × 15 steps)   ★

In the preparation period for many sports, sprints are elementary parts of the training. If you want to be fast or maintain/expand speed, you have to train this ability accordingly.

Due to the high loads, the warm-up program is particularly important. In addition to classic running ABC and coordination exercises, stair runs are a good choice. Here, too, the 1-1 technique is the main technique.

Towards the end of the warm-up program, you can also activate the speed component by not touching every step, but touching every third step—that is, you skip two steps. This way you need less speed and more strength and can train an explosive start, for example.

9.3 Stair Running Sessions for Beginners and Athletes

The following sessions are suitable for beginners to stair running, both to participate in stair running competitions later on and to improve performance in other sports (e.g., soccer, handball, beach volleyball).

Intuition is the best indicator for choosing the right session. What appeals to you? Try it out and then decide whether there will be another session with this sequence or another sequence is more appealing. If you know your training goal and want to improve specifically, choose the session that is most useful for that.

5 × 5 Floors With Breaks as Short as Possible

Procedure: Run quickly up the stairs and then come slowly, step by step, back down—and then run back up again.

Technique: Use the 1-1, 2-1, or 2-2 technique.

Training goal: Achieve a high load to increase your load tolerance at high intensities (short and sharp, comparable to HIIT training [high-intensity interval training])

Break: Go back down the steps quickly.

8–10 × 5 Floors With 80 Percent Effort and Short Breaks

Procedure: Run slowly, step by step, up and down each time.

Technique: Use the 1-1 or 2-1 technique.

Training goal: This exercise increases endurance capacity by increasing the load over a longer period of time.

Rest: Walk quickly back down the steps.

VARIATION

Use the 2-2 technique. With the 2-2 technique you are using a noticeably greater amount of strength. Speed and quickness are reduced.

6 × 5 Floors Full Throttle With Long Pause ★★

Procedure: Run up the stairs at maximum speed, slowly descend one step at a time plus one minute of additional recovery.

Technique: Use the 1-1 or 2-2 technique.

Training goal: The goal is a very high load to increase your load tolerance in the high load range and develop speed plus coordination (short and sharp, comparable to HIIT training).

Break: Walk down the steps and run on the flat if necessary.

EXPERT TIP

Walk two minutes in between on the flat and keep your body moving. Recovery is faster than if you stand or sit still, although mentally, it's a little more challenging to keep moving.

5–12 × 5 Floors Walking Quickly ★

Procedure: Walk quickly up and down the stairs.

Technique: Use the 1-1 or 2-1 technique.

Training goal: The workout is less intense and therefore trains (high) aerobic endurance. This session is suitable for pre-season training, especially in winter/spring if it is slippery and cold outside.

Rest: Walk down the steps.

VARIATION 1
Walk without touching the handrail. This strengthens and tones the legs and uses other muscles, such as the core and lateral leg muscles, compared to using the arms on the handrail.

VARIATION 2
Use the 2-2 technique. Walking slowly increases the amount of strength in the movement because the dynamics and momentum are missing. This way you train your leg strength while walking slowly, especially if you don't use the handrail. The proportion of strength additionally increases with smaller body size.

Walk 5 × 5 Floors

Procedure: Walk quickly up and down the stairs. Take two or three steps per step, leaving one or two steps untouched.

Technique: Use the 2-2 or 3-3 technique.

Training goal: By walking slowly, the session becomes an intense training session for your strength. This training effect becomes stronger when you increase the stride length from two to three steps (i.e., change from the 2-2 to the 3-3 technique). This change is suitable for experienced athletes, as technique and stability in the torso must be maintained.

Pause: Walk down the steps quickly.

5 × 5 Floors With Rhythm Change

Procedure: Start with one step per stride and change to two steps (leaving one step untouched) and again to one step and so on. Change rhythm and technique on each landing (i.e., after 6–10 steps).

Technique: Use the 2-1 technique.

Training goal: By changing the rhythm, in addition to physical performance, mental training is also achieved. The fast switching of running technique under high load is challenging for concentration and coordination after a few intervals.

Rest: Walk down the steps quickly.

VARIATION
Make the breaks rather longer to maximize recovery. At the beginning of the preparation for a season, the longer breaks can also be necessary and helpful because the basic endurance is not yet well developed.

Pyramid (Five, four, three, two, one, two, three, four, five floors) ★★

Procedure: Run up the stairs at maximum speed, slowly descend one step at a time.

Technique: Use the 1-1 or 2-2 technique.

Training goal: The alternating lengths of the stairs vary the load and the running speed. Thus, the session includes several elements—and towards the end also a willpower training, when it gets exhausting.

Rest: Walk down the steps quickly.

VARIATION
More focus on speed is created by inverting the pyramid and starting and ending with one floor. At the same time, this variation can be used to have a lower load.

10 STAIR JUMPS

Why would anyone train stair jumps?

A fair question, especially if you've experienced how demanding and tiring this can be. But that's exactly where the treasure is hidden. A deeper look into the structure of jumps reveals that strength and speed are trained particularly strongly. Depending on the exercise, coordination is added. Those who jump for longer periods will also generate an endurance effect on the muscles. However, when it comes to stair jumps, due to the higher load: More is not always better!

You need a sense of proportion in order not to get into a physical overload. With this measured approach, the overload irritations and injuries that are widespread in elite and leisure sports can be avoided.

Depending on how jumps are integrated into the training, different goals can be achieved. In the main and middle part of the training session, jumps have the goal of improving your skills. For the cool-down, jumps are not well suited due to the increased load. In addition, the already accumulated fatigue of the body and muscles hinders the actual adaptation effect of jumps.

10.1 Warm-Up: Start of the Training Session

The activation of the muscles, the cardiovascular system, and the central nervous system are the main components of every warm-up. You get yourself physically and mentally ready for the following workout in the main part of the session.

In addition to improving performance, the main goal of the warm-up is to reduce the risk of injury. For these reasons, jumps can be used at a lower intensity at the beginning of the workout. This can be achieved by selecting jumps with a lower load and reducing the intensity.

10.1.1 Positive Effects

Those who are used to warming up with a pure endurance program will quickly notice the differences.

1. Activation of the musculature

The extremely short, more intensive loads of the jumps wake up the muscle and prepare it to perform. The muscles used are supplied with more blood; tendons, ligaments, and fasciae are activated. This occurs through the rather jerky load, with which a slight pulling and stretching stimulus is applied to the structures.

2. Activation of mental readiness

During jumps, it is difficult to drift off into your thoughts. It takes focus and thus the athlete achieves a faster and stronger focus through the jumps in the warm-up, which supports the training for the further exercises. The short, intense loads also bring the nervous system into a heightened state of activity to build on in the following training session.

10.2 Main Part of the Training Session

Faster, higher, further is the goal of training as a whole and thus of many training sessions. If stair runs are on the schedule, this goal should be targeted consciously, because stair intervals are legendary in other sports for a reason.

You can use this blasting power to get to a higher performance level, have more confetti and fun in training or, if you overdo it, pulverize your foundation

All this does not happen immediately, but requires several sessions, preferably building on each other, with a combination of stair runs and stair jumps. For this, the section with the training plans gives you practical ideas.

10.2.1 Positive Effects

The effects depend on the particular training and can mainly result in the following adaptations:

1. Increase in speed
With fast jumps, short ground contact times, and the shortest possible reaction time, the effect on the organism is designed to activate, use, and therefore train fast muscle fibers. To achieve this effect, you need maximum recovery with maximum motivation; these are the basic requirements for any speed training, even with stair jumps.

2. Increase in coordination
Due to the given stride length, there is a parameter that is unfamiliar to many athletes. Whether on the grass, the tartan track, or in the hall, the step length can be freely chosen. On the stairs it's different and that's what demands more attention and concentration. This means you need more coordination in your legs, arms, and overall body muscles. Complex sequences of exercises and jumps can further increase this effect.

3. Increase in strength and strength endurance
By overcoming the given height difference, stair jumps always have a higher strength component, compared to flat running. This has a positive training effect on the strength values. This effect is particularly strong in the case of intensive jumps (e.g., deep squats or jumps over many steps).

EXPERT TIP

In addition to concentric force development, in which the muscle shortens under load, there is eccentric force development, in which the muscle lengthens under load. The classic example of eccentricity is running downhill or down the stairs. According to current studies, this type of training is more intensive than concentric force development.

In practical terms, this means

Stairs/mountain up: Cardiovascular system = very strenuous | muscular = demanding.

Stairs/downhill: Cardiovascular system = strenuous | muscular = highly demanding.

4. Increase the willpower

The jumps are very demanding on both the body and the mind. With each jump the exhaustion increases. You can take advantage of this effect and train your willpower. It is important to have the focus and attention to perform the jumps technically correct.

10.3 Exercises for Stair Jumps

This chapter is designed for your practical training on the stairs. It explains how to perform the jumps. However, make sure you think for yourself, because no exercise can be explained so precisely that everything is clear. Try to understand the idea and goal behind each exercise and feel into your body. Stair jumps unfold their effect with a time delay:

1. After you're done with your set of jumps, the perceived load continues to increase. For example, individual muscles may vibrate, twitch, or cramp.

2. After the session, you may notice how the muscles vibrate and twitch when you lift a glass or sit, etc. These are all personal experiences of mine or other athletes, and by no means does everyone experience them. But if you feel like it, you now have an idea of how hard you can run. If that doesn't appeal to you, keep moderation in the exercises, start slow, and gradually increase. This is the best advice, because it allows the muscles, tendons, and ligaments to adapt.

Theory is good, practice is better.

In a few minutes on the stairs you can train both strength and coordination, and with a few more repetitions your endurance. It doesn't need skyscrapers, a few steps or floors are enough. Every human being has the ability to learn and adapt skills through imitation and observation; take this chance and make it easier for yourself to get started by watching the videos in the following chapters via the QR codes.

Note: Of course I'm also happy if you give feedback in the form of a comment this way.

To stream the following videos, simply scan the QR code with your cell phone, either with an app or the camera. For some e-readers, you can simply tap the QR code.

One Step, Double-Leg Jump ★

Starting position:

Stand in front of the first step with your legs shoulder-width apart.

Exercise description:

Extend your knees and hop up one step. The movement comes only from the ankle joints; the knee and hip joints are fixed as much as possible. You can keep your hands on your hips. Overall, ensure an upright, stretched posture during the exercise.

Reps: Perform 5-10 jumps in a row.

Rest: Walk back and focus briefly before the next round.

Sets: Start with 3-5 rounds.

Training effect: You strengthen your calf muscles, which gives you greater potential for stair, road, and mountain running and cycling.

 Scan here for the video

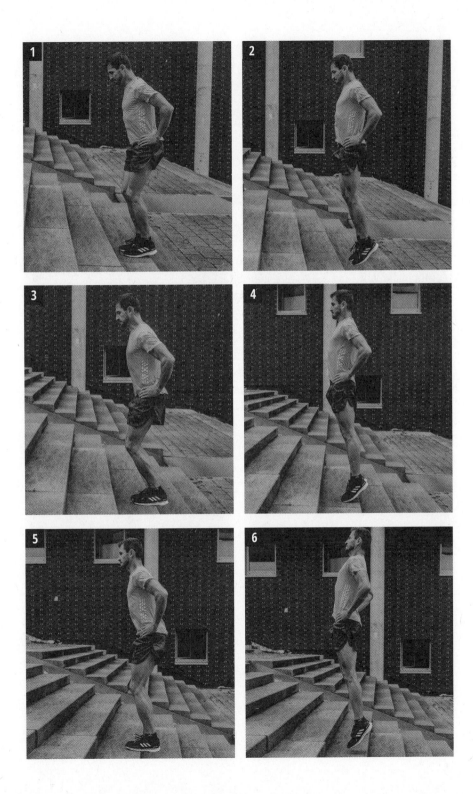

Two Steps, Double-Leg Jump ★★

Starting position:

Stand in front of the first step with your legs shoulder-width apart.

Exercise description:

Bend your knees slightly and hop up two steps, leaving one step untouched. The movement comes from the ankles and knees or from the calf and thigh muscles. The hands and arms support your movement by bringing them back as you squat slightly and bringing them forward quickly as you jump.

Tip: Swing your arms in reverse from front to back on your next jump. The more you land on your midfoot, the more you work your calf muscles.

Reps: Perform 4–8 jumps in a row.

Rest: Walk back and focus for a moment before the next round.

Sets: Start with 3–5 rounds.

Training effect: You strengthen the calf and leg muscles. In addition, the use of the arms trains the coordination and the arm muscles.

Scan here for the video

Three or More Steps, Double-Leg Jump ★★★

Starting position:

The starting position is the same as in the exercise before.

Exercise description:

Squat lower to get more momentum from the arms.

Reps: Perform 4–8 jumps in a row.

Rest: Walk back and focus for a moment before the next round.

Sets: Start with 3-5 rounds.

Training effect: You intensively strengthen the calf and leg muscles. In addition, the use of the arms trains coordination and the arm and shoulder muscles.

One Step, Double-Leg Jump ★

Starting position:

Stand in front of the steps with your legs slightly more than shoulder-width apart and bend your knees to about 45 degrees.

Exercise description:

From a quarter squat or half squat, jump up one step with both legs. Land on the midfoot so you can jump directly into the next step. Keep your arms in front of your body as you would in a squat. Alternatively, swing your arms from front to back and then from back to front on the next jump.

Reps: Perform 8–15 jumps in a row.

Rest: Walk back.

Sets: Start with 3–5 rounds.

Training effect: Strengthening of the front thigh muscles due to the constant load in the light squat.

Two or More Steps, Double-Leg Jump ★★

Starting position:

Stand in front of the steps with your legs slightly wider than shoulder-width apart and bend your knees to about 45 degrees.

Exercise description:

From the quarter squat or half squat, jump up one step with both legs. Land on the midfoot so that you can make the next jump directly. Keep your arms in front of your body as you would for a squat. Alternatively, you can swing your arms from front to back and then from back to front on the next jump.

Reps: Perform 5–10 jumps in a row.

Rest: Walk back.

Sets: Start with 3–5 rounds.

Training effect: You will strengthen the front thigh muscles by the constant load in the light squat. By jumping as many steps as possible, you will increase your maximum strength.

  Scan here for the video– Two steps

Scan here for the video– Three steps

Lunges and Jumps to the Side ★

Starting position:

Stand in front of the first step with a lunge. Your body alignment and gaze direction are parallel to the first step.

Exercise description:

From the lunge position, jump up one step with both legs simultaneously. During this sideways movement, keep a constant low hip position and make sure your upper body is upright. Arms are in step position, meaning the left leg is in front and the right arm is at the back position.

Tip: Change the direction of your gaze after each sequence. If you have a weak side, train the weak leg more, in a ratio of 1:2, to reduce the imbalance.

Reps: Perform 5-12 jumps in a row.

Rest: Walk back plus change legs and direction of gaze.

Sets: Start with 3-5 rounds.

Training effect: You strengthen the calf and leg muscles. Due to the lunge, the load on the rear and front thigh muscles is significantly higher.

One Step, Single-Leg Jump

Exercise description:

Bend the knee slightly and jump up one step with the standing leg. The movement comes from the ankle and the knee or from the calf and thigh muscles. The hands and arms support your movement by bringing one arm back and the other arm forward. When you jump with the left leg, the right arm points forward and the left arm backward, as in the running movement.

Tip: Swing your arms back to the starting position after each jump. Alternatively, you can let the arms hang, then the coordination will be easier. If you land on your midfoot, you will train your calf muscles more.

Reps: Perform 4–8 jumps in a row.

Rest: Walk back and focus for a moment before the next round.

Sets: Start with 3–5 rounds.

Training effect: You strengthen the calf and leg muscles. In addition, the use of the arms trains the coordination and also the arm muscles. Due to the one-sided load, the trunk muscles counterbalance the movement and are intensively trained.

Scan here for the video

Two Steps, Single-Leg Jump ★★★

Starting position:

Take the same starting position as for the single-legged step jump.

Exercise description:

This exercise is performed the same as the one step single leg jump, but you need more concentration, focus, and strength for this exercise. This exercise is suitable for advanced and professionals.

Tip: Swing your arms back after each jump. Keep mental focus and be aware of what works and what doesn't work.

Arms forward.

VARIATION:

You can swing your arms both forward and backward. The difference is noticeable.

Reps: Perform 4–8 jumps in a row.

Rest: Walk back and focus intensely before the next round.

Sets: Start with 3–5 rounds.

Training effect: You strengthen the calf and leg muscles. Due to the one-sided load, the trunk muscles counterbalance the movement and are intensively trained. Due to the greater height to be overcome, you train your maximum strength.

Arms backward.

Skating Jumps ★

Starting position:

The one-legged jumps are performed diagonally across the stairs from right to left and left to right.

Exercise description:

Jump as far as possible to the lateral outer ends of the steps. If you are using a very wide staircase, jump diagonally across the stairs as far as you can get while maintaining a safe footing on landing.

Start with a normal stair width of 1–1.5 meters and use the possibilities of the large stairs for larger amplitudes as the training progresses. The arm swings in step position with the movement (left leg in front, right arm in front).

Side view

Scan here for the video

VARIATION:

1. Pause briefly after each landing, find your balance, and focus on the next jump.

2. Not only bring the foot next to the standing foot, but bring the foot slightly beyond the standing foot. It is important to keep your hips straight and stable.

Reps: Perform 5–10 jumps in a row.

Rest: Walk back.

Sets: Start with 3–5 rounds.

Training effect: In addition to strengthening the muscles, the lateral loading effect trains stabilization in the ankle joint.

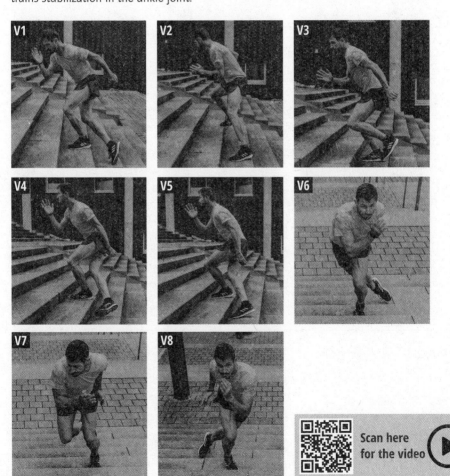

Scan here for the video

Up-Down-Up Stair Jumps

With these jumps you lengthen short stairs. In addition, you use your muscles in an eccentric load in addition to the usual concentric type (your thigh contracts and lifts your body up). When you jump down the stairs, your thigh muscle must lengthen under load (eccentric).

You can do this exercise in many variations. For single leg jumps, you should change your jumping leg after each round.

Exercise description:

Jump with both legs at the same time.

Jump up two steps — jump down one step.

Jump up three steps — jump down one step.

Jump up four steps — jump down two steps.

Reps: Perform 5-14 jumps in a row.

Rest: Walk back.

Sets: Start with 3-5 passes.

VARIATIONS:

1. In the exercises you can do each jump separately and then stop.

2. You can jump in a fluid motion, without stops.

3. Vary the frequency from slow to faster.

4. Perform the jumps in a half squat position and maintain knee flexion during landing.

Overall

An entire stair jumping unit can be designed with these different exercises of up-down jumps. In doing so, the intensity is particularly high for individual muscles. For game athletes, this can be helpful to improve jumping strength, speed, and speed endurance.

 Scan here for the video

 Scan for variation with three steps

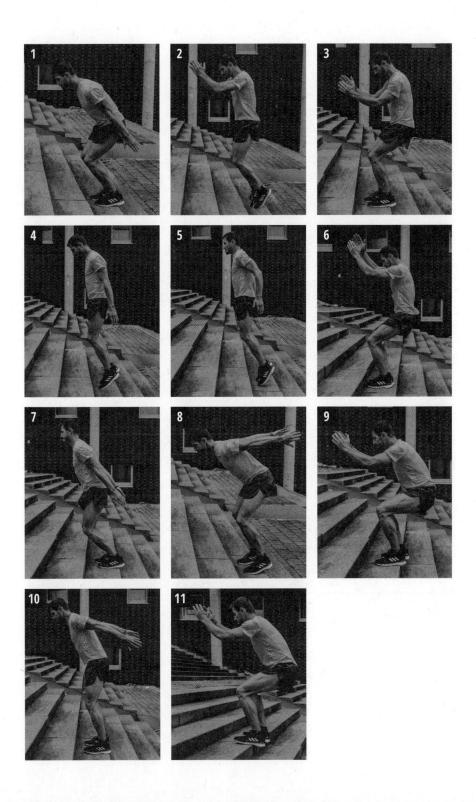

Jump Runs: A Full-Body Workout ★ ★ ★

When mixing stair running and jumping, it is especially important to use your arms. With your arms you support the jump runs and they become easier or you manage more steps per step. In addition, the more fluid motion reduces the risk of injury.

Make sure your arms move in a crossed motion, just like in normal running—that is, when your right foot is in front, your left arm is in front, and vice versa.

The contact times on the steps are slightly longer than when running stairs. Still, you don't stop, as you do with some stair jumps. It's just a momentary delay after each landing phase before you continue jumping.

Exercise description:

You can do this exercise by touching every other step. It will be much more challenging with three steps and four steps. This will only be possible for very few athletes. While the number of steps is secondary, be sure to perform the exercise correctly (e.g., arm work, upright torso, foot strike on the mid/forefoot).

Reps: Perform 5-12 jumps in a row.

Rest: Run back.

Sets: Start with 3-5 passes.

  Scan here for the video

11 COORDINATION EXERCISES ON THE STAIRS

The basic sport motor skill of coordination is a central prerequisite for many movement processes, from game sports to endurance sports. That's why there are countless coordination exercises that develop their full effect when they involve a new movement stimulus for the body and the nervous system. Coordination exercises on the stairs are therefore suitable for all athletes—whether for fun and testing or to improve coordination.

11.1 Integrating Into Your Training

As a rule, these exercises are performed after the warm-up so that the muscles are supplied with blood and ready for more demanding challenges. Through the coordination exercises you activate your nervous system more intensively. This can be helpful in the following main part of the training session (e.g., game variations, sprints or longer intervals). In addition, the higher activation of the body reduces the risk of injury.

Skipping

Exercise description:

Run up the stairs in the usual technique, lifting the knees to a 90-degree angle or higher at the hips. The foot lands on the front part of the foot. Make sure your upper body stays upright and arms swing along as if running.

Reps: 15–30 steps

Rest: Walk back and switch legs if necessary during the variation.

Sets: Start with 3–5 rounds.

VARIATION:

Lift only one knee and run asynchronously. For example, you always lift the right knee and the left knee remains in the normal stair running position.

 Scan here for the video

Double Skips

Exercise description:

The exercise works like skipping. The difference is that on each step you add a small intermediate jump. With this variation, if you are good at normal skipping, you can add a new stimulus.

Reps: 15–30 steps

Rest: Return to the starting point.

Sets: Start with 3–5 rounds.

Scan here for the video

Up-Down Runs ★★

Starting position:

You can run this exercise in the 1-1 technique. If you want to use other stair techniques, you will notice that they are highly demanding in coordination and require intensive preparation.

Exercise description:

Start in front of the first step and run up two steps and directly down one step. Sounds easy and it is—if you have a little practice.

VARIATIONS:

- Run up two steps and down one step.

- Run up three steps and down one step.

- Run up four steps and down two steps.

Reps: 15–30 steps up, plus the same number of steps down

Rest: Return to the starting position and change the starting leg.

Sets: Start with 3-5 runs.

  Scan here for the video

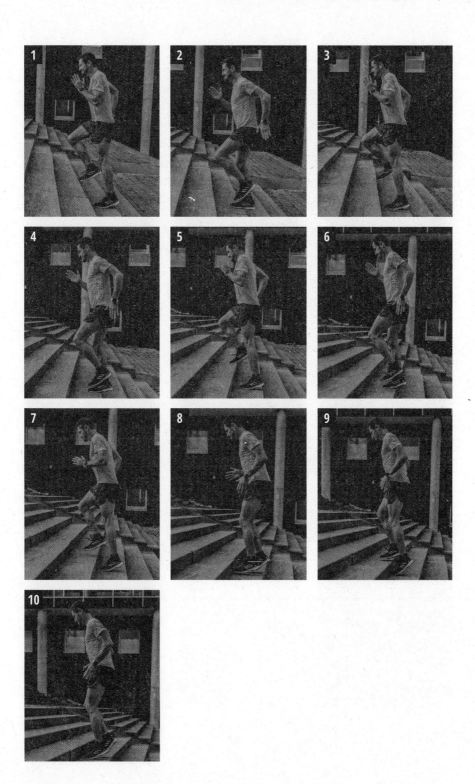

Run Behind and Cross Over   ★ ★

Exercise description:

Jump up one step with the first foot (e.g., with the left foot). After landing, bring the right foot sideways BEHIND the left supporting leg. Push off with the left leg and place the left foot BEHIND the right leg. Then the right leg goes forward one step normally and lands in the normal position in front of and next to the left leg on the fourth step. From then on the sequence starts with the other leg (e.g., the right leg).

This exercise looks dynamic and challenging when done on flat terrain. On stairs it is useful to walk the step sequence first and then dance up the steps.

Reps: 15–30 steps

Rest: return plus change legs and direction of gaze.

Sets: Start with 3–5 rounds.

Scan here for the video

Bounce Jumps

Exercise description:

Raise one leg about 90 degrees at the hip with the foot over the first step. Drop the lifted foot and leg down and make a very small jump with the standing leg so that both feet touch the ground again at the same time. Then, using the reactive force from the impact, jump up one step. The leg that was bent now makes a small jump, while you pull the other leg up to 90 degrees at the hip and let it fall down onto the stairs from this position.

Reps: 10-20 steps

Rest: Return.

Sets: Start with 3-5 rounds.

Walking Backwards Up the Stairs

Important: Recommended only for deep steps!

Exercise description:

A simple exercise is to walk up the stairs backwards. This works well if the steps are one and a half to twice as deep as your feet are long. Less step depth increases the risk of twisting your ankle.

VARIATIONS:

If you are more experienced, you can take two or more steps per stride. The difficulty of walking up the stairs increases significantly with each extra step per stride.

Reps: 10-20 steps

Rest: Return to starting position.

Sets: Start with one run.

Scan here for the video

Walking Backwards Down the Stairs ★

Exercise description:

The foot lands on the mid-foot, preferably in the middle of the step, where it should feel good to you. This exercise can also be used in addition to other exercises for walking down the stairs. Pay special attention that the arms move opposite to the legs (i.e., when the right leg goes backwards, the right arm goes forward).

Reps: 10–20 steps

Rest: Return to starting position.

Sets: Start with one run.

 Scan here for the video

Two Contacts per Step ★

Exercise description:

Touch each step with each foot, which means two contacts per step. This exercise is ideal to train speed and frequency. Use your arms to control the frequency through the arm swing; keep it high if necessary. Also, at very high frequency, keep the upper body upright and stay loose. Many runners have a tendency to bend in at the hips.

Reps: 10–20 steps

Rest: Return and run a few meters flat.

Sets: Start with 3–5 runs.

 Scan here for the video

1-2-1-2 Contacts per Step

Exercise description:

Touch the first step normally. Touch the second step with one foot and then with the other. Touch the third step normally, and the fourth step again with two contacts.

Example:

Step 1: Left

Step 2: Right, left

Step 3: Right

Step 4: Left, right

Reps: 9–27 steps

Rest: Return to starting position.

Sets: Start with 3–5 rounds.

Scan here for the video

1-2-3-2-1 Contacts per Step ★★★

Exercise description:

Touch the first step normally. Touch the second step with one foot and then with the other foot. Touch the third step with three foot contacts. Touch the fourth step with two contacts, and the last step with one contact.

Example:

Step 1: Left

Step 2: Right, left

Step 3: Right, left, right

Stage 4: Left, right

Stage 5: Left

Stage 6: Same as step 1, but continue with right

Reps: 9–27 steps.

Rest: Return.

Sets: Start with 3–5 rounds.

EXPERT TIP

The changing number of stairs per step changes the frequency and the use of force. By using the arms more intensively or faster, the exercise becomes easier and more intense at the same time.

  Scan here for the video

Butt Kicks

Exercise description:

Pull the heel towards the buttocks so that you feel tension on the front side of the thigh. It is important that your upper body is upright and that you move your arms in the running motion. The arms can help keep the rhythm. Each time you lift the heel, you move your foot up one step.

Reps: 10–20 steps

Rest: Return to the starting position.

Sets: Start with 3–5 rounds.

Scan here for the video

12 STRENGTHENING EXERCISES ON THE STAIRS

The human body has 656 muscles, which are divided into smooth and transversely stiffened muscles. The smooth muscles surround organs and are controlled by the subconscious. The approximately 400 transversely striated skeletal muscles can be controlled voluntarily—and therefore strengthened. We use many of the muscles not individually, but in combination.

The most important combination is that of agonist and antagonist. The former performs the movement, the latter reverses the movement. A simple example is when you tense the biceps and the arm bends, then you tense the triceps and the arm stretches back to the starting position. This is how almost all joints and muscles work.

"Normal" is for the muscles to be balanced against each other in their performance; if there is an imbalance, irritation and injury will occur.

Strengthening exercises serve to mitigate and resolve imbalances when you train some individual muscles and muscle groups more and stronger than others. For this purpose, if you are muscularly balanced, you can train agonist and antagonist and therefore become more powerful overall.

In a complex movement like running stairs, hundreds of muscles in the body are involved—some of them very intensively like the calf, thigh, and back muscles. Therefore, exercises to strengthen the muscles are recommended as a balance or to increase performance. The exercises listed focus on performance growth. For muscle growth, the number and intensity of the exercises should be different.

The stairs are particularly suitable for strengthening exercises because the difference in height allows different exercises and the intensity can be varied.

Calf Raise Plus Variations

Starting position:

Stand with the front of the foot on the edge of the first step; only the balls of the feet touch the step, the heels are in the air.

Exercise description:

Push yourself up on your toes and hold the position at the highest point for 1–3 seconds. Then lower your heel as far as possible, preferably below the edge of the step, until you feel a stretch in your calves. Push up as quickly as possible from the low position and hold before slowly lowering.

Reps: 3–8 calf raises

Rest: Rest one minute between rounds.

Sets: Start with 2-4 rounds.

Training effect: Achilles tendon and calf muscles are trained.

VARIATIONS:

1. The exercise becomes more difficult when you take both legs at the same time without holding on (see picture).

2. The exercise becomes much more challenging when you perform the exercise with one leg at a time.

3. The exercise becomes more challenging if you throw a ball up or against a wall at the same time.

Climbers   ★ ★ ★

Starting position:

Put one foot on the first step. Touch the step at the heel.

Exercise description:

Try to pull yourself up with as much force as possible from the upper leg. At the same time, the upper leg remains almost fully extended. This way the power of the ascent is generated from the back thigh/hamstrings and you have a strong training stimulus there. Change legs every step.

Note: This exercise is highly effective and efficient if you perform it correctly. Make sure that you feel the load in the back thighs during the exercise and that you start with few repetitions to avoid too much muscle soreness.

Reps: 7–15 steps

Rest: Return to the starting position.

Sets: 1–4 rounds

Training effect: The hamstring muscles are trained.

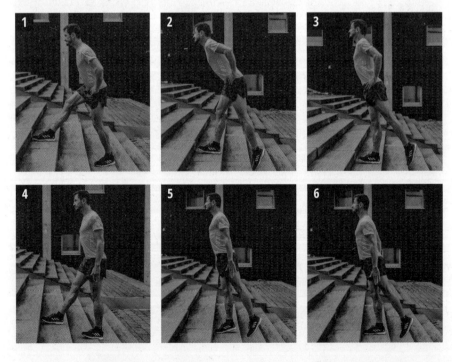

Walk as Many Steps as Possible

Exercise description:

Stand in front of the first step. Take a really big step, as many steps as possible. Tall people manage to take four or even five steps per step. Note that you only take two or three steps on the first one and increase after that. This gives you a good chance of avoiding overload. The goal is to target your maximum strength and make yourself stronger.

Reps: 3–8 steps

Rest: Return to starting position.

Sets: Start with 2–3 rounds.

Training effect: The anterior thigh muscles are trained.

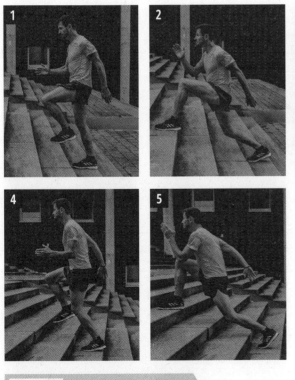

Scan here for the video

Floor Scale Plus   ★★★

Starting position:

Stand with one leg on the first step, facing across the stairs. Lean forward while keeping the other leg an extension of the body.

Exercise description:

Bend forward so that the upper body is parallel to the floor; this requires sufficient flexibility in the rear thigh muscles. The standing leg is extended and the arms are pressed into the hips. Hold this position for 2–5 seconds. Then move the upper body back to an upright position and make a jump with the standing leg to the next step.

Reps: 8–15 steps

Rest: Walk back and change the direction of the gaze and the standing leg.

Sets: Start with 2–4 passes.

Training effect: The rear thigh muscles are trained.

VARIATION:

It's a little easier if you don't jump up one step with your standing leg, but with the other leg. This can be helpful in the beginning.

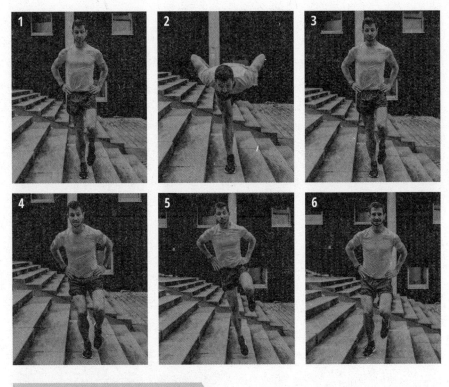

  Scan here for the video

Step–Sit ★★

Exercise description:

Jump down one step and lower the buttocks to the step one step higher. Make sure your knees stay behind an imaginary line above your toes. The lower leg is vertical when lowering. The weight is distributed over the entire sole of your foot, both heel and forefoot. Stretch the arms forward in front of your body for support, if necessary. Alternatively, you can let them hang or cross them in front of your chest. After squatting down, stand up again with the same movement. Once you are standing completely, jump down one more step.

Reps: 8–15 steps

Rest: Walk up.

Sets: Start with 2–4 rounds.

Training effect: The front thigh muscles are trained.

EXPERT TIP

Use this exercise in combination with a climbing exercise. This will increase the intensity and challenge of your workout.

Scan here for the video

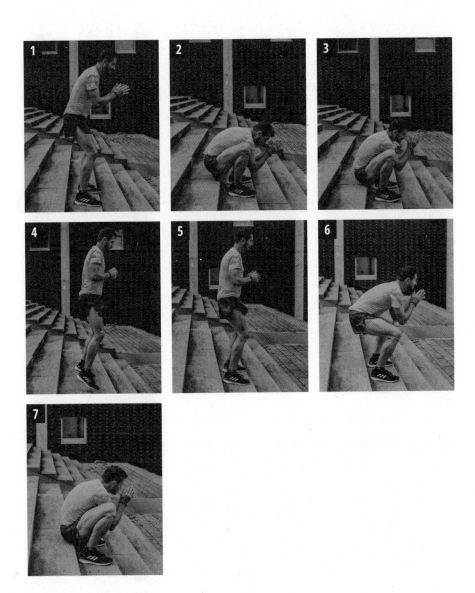

Stair Climber ★

Starting position:

Get into the quadruped position: feet are in front of the first step, hands are positioned on the third, fourth, or fifth step, depending on your height.

Exercise description:

Support yourself on the stairs with both hands. The hands are three or four steps higher than the legs. Begin a walking motion with your legs. Make sure your hips are as straight as possible and your buttocks are close to the floor. This will give you a stronger workout of the core muscles.

Reps: Perform the exercise for 10–30 seconds.

Rest: Return and change the starting arm and leg.

Sets: Start with 2–4 rounds.

Training effect: Focus on strengthening the trunk.

VARIATION:

Perform the exercise in slow motion to train the postural muscles more.

 Scan here for the video

Half/Quarter Pistol Squats

Starting Position:

With arms extended, go into a squat supported by your right leg.

Exercise description:

The left leg is extended. Once you are in the half or quarter squat with the right leg, move to the next lower step. Now shift the weight to the left leg. Stand up straight again, lift the right leg off the step, and extend it forward. Go into half or quarter bend with your left leg.

Reps: 8–15 steps

Rest: Return and change the starting leg.

Sets: Start with 2–4 rounds.

Training effect: The front thigh muscles are trained.

Scan here for the video

Shaolin Walk ★

Starting position:

Get into a quadruped stance at the top of the stairs with the feet on the top step and the hands positioned on the third, fourth, or fifth step below.

Exercise description:

Take your left hand and right leg one step forward at a time. As you do this, feel your core muscles tighten more to maintain balance. Now take your right hand and left leg and place them two steps forward. Repeat the same with the other leg and arm.

Reps: 8–15 steps down

Rest: Return and change starting arm and leg.

Sets: Start with 2–4 rounds.

Training effect: Arms, shoulder and trunk are the focus of the workout.

NOTE:

Shaolin monks train their body with this way of walking. In TV programs and online videos you will see that the world-famous Buddhist monks practice these exercises for extremely long distances or time. Running and jumping up the stairs and coming down head first can create stair sessions where they descend a four digit number of steps in this exercise. Some of the steps in the monasteries are very steep, which increases the strain on the arms and shoulders.

EXPERT TIP

Wearing cycling gloves to reduce the strain on the skin on the palms of your hands.

 Scan here for the video— Shaolin Walk

 Scan here for the video— Variation

Push-Up Pyramid ★★

Starting position:

Place your feet in front of the first step, facing away from the steps.

Exercise description:

Get into the push-up position and do a push-up. Then place your feet one step higher and move your hands back a little. Continue this exercise until your hands are directly in front of the first step. Then go back down one step with your feet after each push-up. This creates a small push-up pyramid.

Reps: Go up and down 2–6 steps.

Rest: None.

Sets: Start with 2–4 rounds.

Training effect: Arms and shoulders are trained.

 Scan here for the video

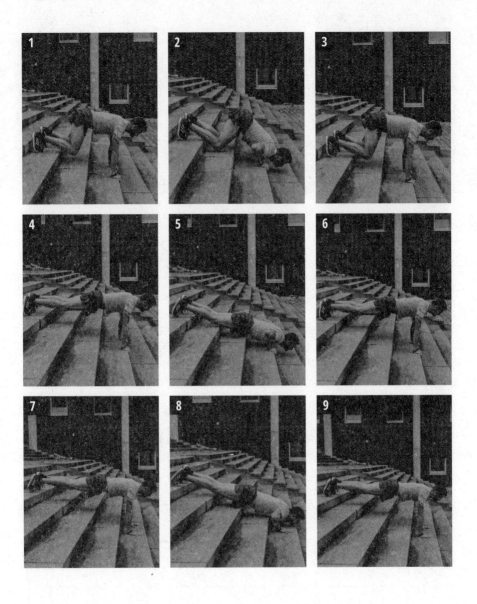

13

STRETCHING EXERCISES ON THE STAIRS

In addition to strengthening, which makes the muscle strong, mobility and flexibility are important to counterbalance. We can see from children who are active and healthy how flexible an adult body should be. This is a benchmark that is ambitious and healthy for many. If you're far from that, no problem.

Build stretching into your workouts and watch your flexibility increase until you are as flexible as you want to be. If you have doubts about whether any of the exercises are right for you, a physiotherapist, osteopath, or a good sports doctor can give you tips and advice.

13.1 Why Do You Need Flexibility?

Your muscles have a working length and this is reduced and limited by imbalances between a muscle and its antagonist. If the agonist and antagonist (e.g., the biceps and triceps) are of different strengths, the weaker muscle reacts with increased tension and feels shortened.

Stretching exercises help to reduce the tension and restore balance. In addition, the increased flexibility of the fascia around the muscle increases mobility in the joint.

13.2 Static and Dynamic Stretching

In static stretching, to avoid muscle reflexes, you slowly put the muscle under tension and hold this position. You can perform these exercises actively on your own or passively, for example, when a physiotherapist stretches you.

In the dynamic approach, the stretching and neutral positions are alternated. The movement from one state to the other should be controlled, mindful, and with full attention to the body and the exercise.

13.3 Proprioceptive Neuromuscular Facilitation (PNF)

This method is classified into contract-relax (CR) and contract-relax-antagonist-contract (CRAC) version, among others.

CR is a stretching method in which you tense a muscle for 3–5 seconds and then stretch it in the relaxation phase.

Exercise: Place your right leg with the heel on a step, chair, or comparable elevation. Move your upper body forward down toward the top of your foot. As soon as you feel a stretch in the hamstrings, stay in this position. Now tense the hamstrings by feeling the heel press into the stair or seat cushion. You will feel the muscles on the back of the thigh harden from the contraction. Hold this tension for 5–10 seconds and relax the muscles. While relaxing the back of the thigh muscle, try to bend a little bit more towards the front and down towards the top of the foot with the upper body. The exercise will be more intense if you stay stretched in the spine and upper body.

From the new position, repeat the process after a pause of 20 seconds and perform this sequence three times.

CRAC works by tensing a muscle, thereby sending a signal to the brain to relax the opponent. Relaxing the opposing muscle is the real goal. For the hamstring, this would mean contracting the front thigh muscle against resistance.

Exercise: Your gaze direction is away from the stairs. The toes of your right leg are one or two steps higher than your extended left leg. Your right leg presses the toes against the step for 15 seconds. Rest for 20 seconds and repeat the exercise a total of three times.

Note: The CR and CRAC methods of stretching are very effective in increasing your flexibility. However, you should only do this type of stretching under guidance, or if you are a very experienced athlete who knows his or her body well. For many exercises, it is helpful to have a physiotherapist who can assist you with PNF stretching and provide the appropriate resistance. Alternatively, a rope or strong Thera-Band® can provide resistance for many muscles.

Which is the better method?

Hardly any other topic has been discussed more intensively in sports science in recent years than this question. That's why there are countless studies about it, which you can easily find on the internet. A reference to a study from the year 2021 can be found in the appendix under References.

EXPERT TIP

Whether at the stair races in New York, London, and Berlin or at the respective world-famous city marathons, the top runners behave very similarly. A few days before the race, directly after arrival, stretching is even more intensive. Both the athletes themselves and the physiotherapists pull on the tendons and muscles—but not quite like in the training phases. Depending on the athlete, 4–7 days before the race, the muscles are only partially relieved of tension. Why?

Because the athlete needs healthy tension and tightness for competition. If an athlete or physiotherapist softly stretches and kneads the muscles the day before the race, the competition will be just as tensionless. Anyone who has ever had an intensive massage knows how relaxed and often tired you feel afterwards. The muscle wants a lot, but certainly not to run up the stairs at full speed.

That's why the closer the race gets, the less stretching is done and the more dynamic the mobilization exercises become—a short stretch in and out of the muscle. In this way, the muscle retains tension and the athlete feels good. This is a behavior that can be observed in many athletes in all sports immediately before the start of the race.

There are no studies on what happens or why athletes do this. No professional would want to study this in the seconds before the starting shot. That's why a lot of research goes unnoticed and only one specific aspect gets attention, usually with not-so-successful athletes, and that's why I recommend that you observe your body in addition to gaining knowledge from books and studies. Every body and every athlete is different and therefore you know yourself best.

13.4 How Long Should You Stretch?

This depends on your goal. If you want to increase your flexibility, it works especially well if you hold the exercises for at least 20 seconds, better if you hold them 30–40 seconds. Only after a few seconds do adhesions around the muscles begin to loosen. This then allows for greater mobility in the joints. In the literature this is described as increasing the range of motion.

It will take weeks and months before you feel a lasting and noticeable change in your range of motion in the joints. Progress occurs more quickly during non-training periods because the temporary contra-effects of training are eliminated. It makes the most sense to make stretching a part of your training to continuously improve your mobility.

13.5 Mobilization With Stretching Exercises

When stretching exercises are performed with little intensity and only very short stretches are performed, an effect of mobilization occurs in the body. By moving the muscles and fasciae you get a feeling of relaxation and greater mobility. The effect is therefore similar to a light massage and stimulates regeneration.

Many athletes do mobilization with light stretching exercises before competitions or hard sessions.

At competitions, you often see athletes doing a quick stretching exercise just before the starting gun goes off —briefly into the stretch and directly out again. This takes one, two, three seconds and therefore has a different effect than stretching.

Mobilization is not a substitute for true stretching, which involves holding the position for at least 20 seconds.

Stretching During Intensive Stair Sessions

After an intense workout, it is recommended to perform stretching exercises a few hours later or the next day. The reason for this is that stretching puts additional strain on the muscle. If you have been working out intensively, it is counterproductive to stretch intensively. Mobilization exercises are better.

Before intense stair running sessions, it helps the body to be active, ready, and mobile for the steps if you do some stretching exercises as mobilization.

The exercises are described for static performance. All exercises can also be done dynamically. To do this, go through the exercise as described, alternating between stretching and returning to the neutral position.

If you notice strong differences in the mobility of the sides of the body, it is recommended to do the exercises with the immobile, mobile side and again with the immobile side. In this way the sides will equalize over time.

Lunge | Hip Flexors

Starting position:
Stand with your back to the stairs and place your left foot two or more steps lower. Keep the upper body upright and the hands on the hips.

Exercise description:
Bring the hips toward the ground by bending the left leg more. Make sure the knee of the left leg does not push over an imaginary vertical line above the toes of the foot. If necessary, place the left foot a little further away from the stairs. Then perform the exercise with the other leg.

VARIATIONS:

1. The exercise will be more intense if you lean your upper body backwards during the stretch.

2. Turn to face the stairs and put the front leg 2–4 steps higher and perform the exercise the other way around.

Training effect: The hip flexor is one of the strongest muscles in the body. It lifts your leg high and therefore it is used intensively when climbing stairs. When it is shortened, it is harder to run upright and runners fall more easily into a forward lean position which means more stress on the thighs.

Even when running flat, you need length in the hip flexor to be able to take big strides and bring the leg far behind the body when pushing off the ground.

Hamstrings ★

Starting position:

Stand in front of the first step and place the heel of the right foot on the second, third, or fourth step. If you feel no stretch during the exercise, raise the leg one step higher. The standing leg is stretched.

Exercise description:

Bend forward from the hips until you feel the stretch in the back of the thigh. Keep your hips stable and parallel. You can place your hands on your hips or on your thighs. Then perform the exercise with the other leg.

VARIATION:

Hold the foot of the stretched leg and pull it towards you. This will give you an additional stretch in the back of the lower leg.

Training effect:

The hamstrings are often too weakly developed. The reaction of the muscle with increased tension leads to pain in this area and also to back problems in the lumbar region. This exercise counteracts this by reducing the tension. At the same time, it is a good idea to do strengthening exercises for this muscle (e.g., climbers).

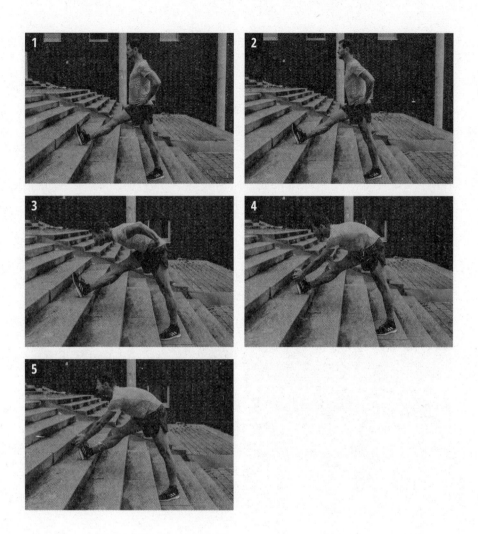

Adductors ★

Starting position:

Stand sideways to the stairs and place the leg closer to the stairs on the second, third, or fourth step. The standing leg is extended.

Exercise description:

Bend your upper body sideways towards the raised foot and feel the stretch stimulus on the inner thigh. You can put your hands on your hips. Then perform the exercise with the other leg.

Training effect:

By reducing the tension in the inner tight, the risk of injury is reduced and at the same time, the performance of the muscle increases when it has its healthy range of motion.

Abductors ★

Starting position:

Stand sideways to the stairs with the foot farther away from the stairs on the first step so that the legs are crossed.

Exercise description:

Bend the upper leg slightly at the knee until you feel tension on the outside of the lower leg. In addition, tilt the upper body away from the stairs until you feel a stretch in the lateral outer thigh muscles of the leg that is in front of the first step. The stretch will be more intense if you now tilt your upper body back toward the stairs. Then perform the exercise with the other leg.

Training effect:

The abductors naturally have a high tension. If it has become too high, you can compensate for it with this exercise and reduce the risk of injury.

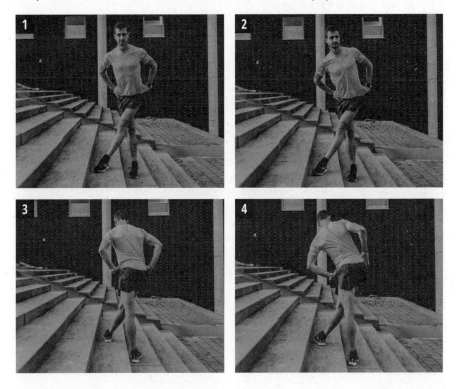

Gluteal Muscles ★

Starting position:

Stand in front of the stairs and place the right leg, bent 90–130 degrees, on the second, third, or fourth step. Hands are next to the foot and next to the knee to support the upper body. The left leg remains extended or slightly bent.

Exercise description:

Lean forward on or over the right leg until you feel the stretch in the gluteus maximus. Then perform the exercise with the other leg.

VARIATION:

With the upper body upright, stretch the hip flexor of the extended leg.

Training effect: By reducing the tension in the muscles, the risk of injury is reduced and at the same time, the performance of the muscle increases when it has its healthy mobility and action length. Moreover, it is a pleasant feeling when the gluteal muscle is relaxed.

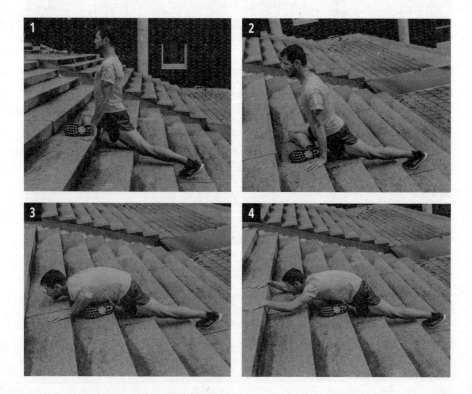

Shoulders

Starting position:

Grasp the railing with both hands about shoulder width apart and bring the upper body towards the floor; the direction of gaze is towards the floor.

Exercise description:

Try to bring the shoulder girdle and chest further towards the floor and feel the tension and compression in the shoulders and muscles. By shifting your weight to the left or right side of the railing, you can increase the stretch in that side.

Training effect:

The shoulder and chest muscles are involved in breathing and therefore need a sufficient range of action. For this reason, this stretching exercise, in addition to giving you more range of motion in the shoulder, also allows you to breathe more easily when the muscles in this area are shortened.

Achilles Tendon and Calf Muscles ★

Starting position:

The feet stand with the front foot on the step, the heel protruding above it. The gaze is directed towards the stairs and the knees are extended.

Exercise description:

The heels are slowly lowered down until an intense stretch is felt in the Achilles tendons.

VARIATIONS:

1. Bend the knees and you will notice the stretch transfer to other areas of the calf muscle.

2. Perform the exercise with only one foot on the floor. If necessary, hold onto the handrail or wall with one hand. This way you increase the stretch of the respective Achilles heel.

Training effect:

This exercise works to solve and prevent Achilles tendon problems.

If the tendon is painful and/or swollen, it is best to consult a physiotherapist or doctor. Often the therapy consists of stretching the tendon despite the pain—which is a very special therapy approach compared to other tendons in the body.

A very dynamic stretching exercise is walking and running backwards. By placing the foot on the forefoot, an active stretching of the Achilles tendon takes place during the rolling motion. Backward running is used as an exercise for both injury therapy and prophylaxis for the Achilles tendon.

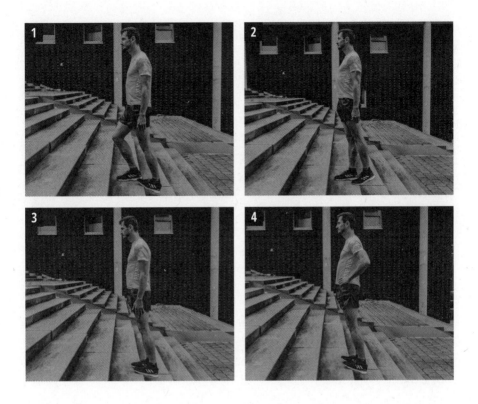

Chest   ★

Starting position:

This exercise requires a wall on which you place the flat of your hand. The arm is stretched horizontally and the gaze is directed towards the wall.

Exercise description:

Slowly turn your gaze, head, and upper body away from the wall and reposition the outer foot until you feel the stretch in the chest and arm. Then perform this exercise with the other arm.

VARIATION:

Stretch the opposing muscles of the chest, opening up your shoulder muscles.

Training effect:

The chest muscles are involved in breathing through the opening of the chest. You feel the difference when you have a slumped, rounded torso compared to an upright torso with an open chest. With the latter, you can breathe more deeply more easily, and that's crucial when running stairs.

In addition, the increased flexibility expands your options for arm pulls on the handrail by allowing you to reach further forward and backward.

INTERVIEW WITH THE KING OF THE STAIRS

Thomas Dold has been outrunning the competition for years, and not just in the Empire State Building!

There are truly nicer places to exercise. The dreary stairwell in the MAINTOWER is definitely not one of them. Nevertheless, it is Thomas Dold's preferred training object. The extreme athlete from Steinach in the Black Forest feels right at home in Frankfurt's skyscraper (240 meters high). Twice a week, the 25-year-old passes through the security gates and races up the 1090 steps to the 52nd floor. Dold is the king of stair climbing. He tells our newspaper in an interview what that means.

Mr. Dold, you have now won the stair race in the Empire State Building for the fifth time in a row, and you have dominated the competition for the last four years. What's the reason?

In the USA, I was just named the Lance Armstrong of the Stairs. I've actually won all the races in the past few years, only coming in second three or four times. One reason for this is that I concentrate fully on these competitions. Mental preparation and day-to-day organization are enormously important.

Don't you also have the right physiognomy?

Certainly. I don't exactly look like the classic 10,000-meter Olympic champion because I have a lot more muscle mass in my thighs and upper arms, which I need for this high-performance sport. Physically, I also have an advantage because I run in lactate zones that would put most people in the hospital.

What do you mean specifically?

At 18 millimol, which was measured years ago, a normal person can no longer move because the muscle cramps. The muscle is then so acidic that the metabolism no longer functions. I can keep up my rhythm until I reach the finish line and run until the muscle is absolutely incapable of moving.

Is that something you can train?

The prerequisite must already be there. But you also have to have the will to defeat your own inner saboteur. During my first run in the Empire State Building, I didn't want to win badly enough. That never happened to me again afterwards. Since then, I've been preparing myself physically, organizationally, and mentally so that I can say I've done everything possible to reach the goal.

That sounds like you have to give up a lot!

No, I'm not giving up anything.

Going to the pub in the evening?

It's rare, but I don't give it up either. The thought that it's the weekend and I have to go out and party doesn't cross my mind at all. Before the race in New York, I would have liked to have done some cross-country skiing, but I postponed that for two weeks out of an abundance of caution.

Do you follow any special diet or nutrition plan?

Should I open my backpack? It's full of buttered bread and fruit. Of course, I don't fill my stomach just before a race. I eat healthy things, but certainly as much as a small family. It's all burned up by my engine. I can eat 500 grams of pasta in the evening by myself, and I also like to have a midnight snack. My father then just shakes his head in disbelief; he can't manage that much all day.

What do your parents say about your extreme professional sport?

They accept it, even if my grandmother can't understand how I can live on it and what I do all day.

Explain it to us.

Just running is not enough. Five victories in New York don't bring anything financially. On the contrary, the prize money doesn't compensate for the high travel costs.

But I am also an entrepreneur with my company and brand RUN2SKY, through which I organize tower runs as training and competitions and sell advertising space. In 2009, I initiated the RUN2SKY Europe tower-running series. I also give keynote speeches.

What kind?

From presentation of the sport to motivational training—whatever is effective for the organizer. There's a difference between telling 150 salespeople about goals, investment, discipline, and motivation, and talking about myself, training, and anecdotes as a kind of entertainer.

What can people learn from you?

Focus on the essentials. Prioritize life. In the morning, I think about what I want to do by the end of the day and get it done.

Sounds like a manager...

(laughs) I have a degree in economics and specialize in controlling, banking, and, above all, marketing. That's what I'm passionate about.

Isn't it a huge effort for you to travel from the Black Forest to Frankfurt for training?

For runners, training usually starts behind the front door. For me, there are three hours in between—an enormous restriction and an obstacle of a financial nature. But if you run the whole thing like a business, you have to account for the arrival and departure under "I" like investments. When I'm on the train, I do a lot of things on my laptop or read, which for nine semesters was often for university.

Do you have keys to every tower in Germany?

(laughs) No. I mainly need a special permit to even get into the stairwell. It took a very long time for the TV tower in Stuttgart, where I was studying at the time, but I still had to go to Frankfurt. In the early years, I even flew to Vienna to train in the Danube Tower because I had been given permission there.

Does the gatekeeper get a case of beer, or how does that work?

You can forget about that. In the MAINTOWER, I talked to more than 20 people on the phone, right up to the top management level, so that in the end I had a number where I could simply call, let them know when I was coming, and that would be fine.

Are you then alone and can train in silence?

In general, yes. In theory, I can run in the MAINTOWER at any time of day or night because it is guarded and accessible 24 hours a day, seven days a week. Most of the thousands of people who work in the tower use the elevators, but every now and then you'll meet someone who walks some of the 52 floors back to their workplace.

What was your most bizarre staircase experience?

When I didn't have the special permits yet, I used to pick tall apartment buildings to practice on. In Tübingen, I looked at a suitable building. A grandmother asked me if I wanted to train here. She could have asked me something. And then she still said: You're not going to jump from the top, are you? When I was able to convince her of the opposite, she even kindly opened the stairwell for me.

Are stairwells all over the world very different from each other?

They are all monotonous, gray, and dusty. The height of the steps varies, as does the number of steps per floor. Sometimes the handrail is made of wood, as in the Empire State Building. There are also large round staircases, for example in the Stuttgart TV Tower; with a triangular floor plan, as in the Frankfurt Trade Fair Tower; or normal rectangular ones.

Don't you get dizzy when you walk closely in the round?

No, it's a routine. Someone who rides a roller coaster twice a week doesn't have any more problems either.

You always wear long black knee socks when you run. Do they make you fast?

(laughs) For sure. The slight pressure on the calf brings a feeling that you just want to start running. Since I struggle with varicose veins, my custom compression socks help me run faster; the blood doesn't pool. But besides that, they are also a bit of a mascot. Whenever I wear the short black ones, it becomes important, a competition is coming up.

What kind of people are stair runners?

Crazy ones, all with tight calves and a firm butt. No, seriously, they're athletes like biathletes, for example, a small group that meets regularly at competitions and travels the world.

How many people do it?

More than 50 and less than 100 people, I guess, who train really hard for it and practice this sport more or less professionally. There are more and more every year.

Who do you have to keep an eye on: the Europeans, the Africans, or the Asians?

Not the Africans; they can't handle the sport and prefer to run more straight. The Australians are very good, they like crazy sports anyway. And in Taipei, there's a little letter carrier who delivers the post in the Taiwanese mountains. (laughs) Actually, it's just two thighs with a person attached to them.

How important is the start?

Enormously important, because it immediately jams at the entrance. Like Michael Schumacher, I also train reaction games to get into pole position immediately at the start or to defend it and be the first to get into the stairwell. I also train not to lose my nerve when I run in fifth. In January in Milan, I overtook a serious opponent in the stairwell for the first time ever. Before that, I was always in front.

How fast do you run up?

My average pace is a good three steps per second. I can climb the 1,576 steps in the Empire State Building in ten minutes and seven seconds. I take two steps at a time until I reach the finish. And I hardly slow down at the end.

Do you go beyond your limit?

(laughs) Of course. I don't lie on the floor for fun when I cross the finish line. I can't do anything anymore, I'm hardly in my right mind, and I'm in a lot of pain.

How many give up?

Almost no one. Those who can't go on, go up slowly. The problem is, you can't stop in the middle like in the Berlin Marathon and get on the subway. You can't get out of the stairwell easily, the floor doors are all locked. So you are faced with the choice of running back or further up to the view to the finish. There the decision is not that difficult.

What is the attraction of running stairs?

Finding out in the shortest possible time what your body can do and even being able to see and feel it afterwards when you approach the top of the barrier and look down. Hardly any other sport pushes you to your physical limits so quickly.

How many competitions do you take part in each year?

It doesn't depend on the season, as it does for a track and field athlete, but I prepare for each race like a boxer. That's why I take part in seven or eight competitions, but those are the biggest international competitions.

You also hold world records in backward running. How does that go together?

Very well. It's like a massage if you mix it gently into your training. And it means prophylaxis against injuries. You train other muscle groups that you wouldn't otherwise need. This prevents muscle imbalance, which can lead to inflammation. Running backwards ensures that I can train harder for much longer. Progress through regression, in a sense.

Where do you run backwards?

It has to be a long flat stretch with no obstacles. What I recommend is to take someone with you who runs in front of you. That's a lot of fun if you can look each other in the eye. It's especially funny when you overtake joggers and look them straight in the eye. They're usually totally surprised and perplexed.

Don't you turn around all the time?

Not anymore. I even run a 3,000-meter race blind. But I used to have to look around every 50 meters.

Where do the competitions take place?

In a normal stadium on the track. It's easy to adjust because you can see the lines. But sometimes also on normal streets, like at the New Year's Eve run in Trier.

Do you dream more of stairs or elevators?

(laughs) Probably both, because I always take the elevator down.

Do you count stairs to fall asleep?

(laughs) No, I prefer to stay with the sheep.

Do you ever take the elevator?

Yes, I do. When I go to the mall, I'd be crazy not to take the escalators or elevator, but to spend half an hour looking for the emergency stairwell, where I might get in but not get out.

Are there any efforts to include stair running or backward running in the Olympic program?

I am not aware of that. That would certainly be attractive, but on the other hand it would not make me happy. When I'm sitting around the table with business economists, I can sell advertising space like no one else. You don't have to charge by the square centimeter, but can do what's effective and efficient. If it came to the Olympics, the possibilities would certainly be limited. Every medal, even the Olympic one, has two sides.

In the world's tallest building, the Burj Khalifa in Dubai, the elevators have been stuck ever since it opened. An image improvement with a staircase race would be just what's needed. Aren't you going to call the sheikh?

You're implying that I haven't tried it yet.

And?

Sure, years ago, when the project was still in the planning stage. But I don't have the necessary connection to get through to the sheikh. And the waiting list for an audience is certainly long. But it remains my goal to either organize a race there or to run it myself. Preferably both.

Maybe the sheik will read this interview and give the green light. Can the tower be done?

Sure it can. I'll just train a bit more. You can't get up to 828 meters anyway; the floors probably end at 600 meters. If I run just five percent slower, my strength will probably last up to 30 percent longer.

Which height has been the top for you so far?

390 meters in Taipei.

Is there a balance to sport for you?

No. Am I supposed to balance out my passion by working in a quarry?

Does someone who shares life with you have to go on the whole racing circus around the world?

No. These events are pleasure for me, but also work. People might think: He's got it good, just jetting around the world and running up stairs. It's not like that. I don't always take a two-week vacation after racing in Taipei. Last time, I left on Thursday and returned early on Monday.

Would your partner be allowed to take the elevator?

(laughs) Sure. She's also allowed to hang out on the sofa when I'm training. But she should also be able to tolerate what I do. And very important: She should share my maxim.

What is it?

Look for solutions and no excuses.

Source: noz.de, February 26, 2010.
Author: Marcus Tackenberg

15 EQUIPMENT

Do you need special shoes for running on the stairs? This question is asked very often, and the answer is what makes running on the stairs so attractive.

No, you can climb stairs with regular running shoes, even regular everyday shoes will do. However, the equipment can be a helpful support factor on your way up and to your goals. Whether physically or mentally, the sports equipment and food industry supports you if you want it.

15.1 Training

15.1.1 Shoes and Cushioning

The most important thing is shoes that fit your feet well. As with any running activity, about a thumb's width of space between the end of the toe and the toe of the shoe is appropriate for stair running. Your retailer will have already explained this to you as this rule also applies to road and trail running.

For the ascent, the cushioning of the shoes plays a secondary role. Your foot strike will not have the impact on the foot and body typical for road running, because you will not hammer the foot from above onto the step, but most likely lift it only minimally higher than the step. Road running is different and therefore cushioning is more important.

However, in some stairwells and outdoor and natural stairs there is the descent to cope with. There it is the other way around and the cushioning should be good and do its job. Many times your body weight acts on your feet and body when descending, especially when you take two or more steps at a fast pace. Likewise, high steps increase the forces acting on your feet as you descend.

Shoes with a thick sole are not recommended. In 2019, shoe manufacturers increasingly began to install very thick soles, including the carbon elements partially integrated in them. Due to the increased center of gravity, large centrifugal forces act, due to the many curves in the staircase. High soles place additional stress on the ankle joints. Flat soles are therefore recommended.

The drop itself is secondary (difference in sole thickness from the heel to the toe), as you will mostly have your heels in the air when climbing. On the descent, you may come up with the heel and benefit from the cushioning. However, it has little effect whether you have a few millimeters more or less forward lean when stepping. It is more important that the cushioning is intact and that you are not wearing old, worn-out shoes. When descending stairs or running downhill, you use the cushioning of your feet, ankles, and calves by placing your feet on the middle part. No shoe can replace this natural cushioning through muscles, tendons, and joints. What you have had since birth is the world's best cushioning.

15.1.2 Practical Shoe Test

The shoe has a certain tension of its own, which you feel when you hold the shoe on the sole and twist it around the longitudinal axis or bend it around the transverse axis. In this way you can see how worn the cushioning is, especially in contrast to new shoes. This test takes a little experience, but then, in addition to your own body feeling, is one of the best tests that you can make independently for the lifetime of the shoe.

15.1.3 Gloves

The most successful stair climber Suzy Walsham, who has won almost every stair race in the world several times, wears gloves. She feels more grip and doesn't have to deal with blisters on her hands.

I know from my own experience that intense pulling on the handrail, especially if you're not used to it, can cause blisters on the palms. This is unlikely with beginners and with only a few floors, but if you run 50, 100, or more floors at full power, swinging around each platform and working with your arms on the handrail to the maximum, intense forces act on the palms of your hands. If you want to avoid this, you should put on gloves.

The disadvantage of this is that you carry a little more weight with you and the feeling is different. That's why most runners run without gloves—also because they don't get blisters due to the low load. The padding on the palms, in addition to the formation of blisters, also prevents you from slipping through very sweaty hands.

Whether road bike, mountain bike, or comparable sports, gloves are best left to the practical self-test. There are no special stair-running gloves.

15.2 Competition

Not everyone wants to run for trophies, victories, and best times. But even as a child, many people loved to compare themselves to others. In sports, unlike many other areas of life, it is allowed to be good and better than oneself or others. Besides, competitions offer the chance to see—far from any excuses—what body and mind can do that day.

In the staircase, which removes many environmental parameters, this focus effect on oneself is even stronger. If you're a runner who is attracted to this, good equipment can help you achieve your goals.

15.2.1 Competition Shoe

Every gram counts, especially when the weight must not only go forward over a flat asphalt runway or tartan track, but also upward at the same time. This is why very light competition shoes are ideal for stair running—but they must still be stable enough to withstand the centrifugal forces in the curves.

There are no special stair-running shoes for both training and competition. That is why, as in other running disciplines, there are very different implementations of the idea of being as light as possible.

1. Barefoot—Tomasz Klinsz at the Donauturm Run-Up in Vienna

I could hardly believe my eyes when I saw Tomasz Klinsz from Poland running barefoot at the 2006 Run-Up. Together with a fellow countryman he ran up the 760 steps of the Danube Tower without a cushioning sole. This alone would not have been worth mentioning here, since there are always barefoot runners. But the stairs at the Danube Tower are not concrete and flat, rather a steel grid construction. One has quite good grip with shoes on the grids. Without shoes probably even more, when the wavy steel sheets dig into the soles of your feet.

Tomasz Klinsz at Altus Tower in Katowice

2. Barefoot Shoes

The Italian sole manufacturer Vibram equipped some tower runners for the premiere of its special shoes, each toe of which is separately enclosed as in a glove. The ultra-thin sole protects against rough bumps and sharp edges. The individually packaged toes are a true eye-catcher.

The grip of the soles is maximum—the foot does not move a millimeter after the touch down. The light upper material of the shoes hold the resulting forces at high cornering speeds, but do not stabilize the ankle and ligaments. Maybe that's why these shoes have not gained widespread acceptance in tower running, even though they are extremely light, have grip, and are a real eye-catcher.

With barefoot shoes you train your foot muscles to a high degree. This results in excellent variety and strengthening of the important foot muscles when running stairs without the hard impact on tarmac and concrete.

Sliding Party at the Tower Run in Chongquing

The stairs and the staircases are a special terrain that differs in every race. After several years of racing experience, I knew many staircases and their special features. Often it was my first time at the start and I had to find my rhythm as quickly and perfectly as possible.

On 14 September 2014, this was one of the most difficult tasks I ever had to solve—and I was lucky.

At the end of the warm-up, I looked at the first steps of the staircase to get a feeling of how best to behave tactically at the mass start.

I noticed that the stairwell had been freshly cleaned and a thin film of soft soap was spread on it. It was impossible to get grip under my soles if I moved just a little faster in the turns.

BANG! The firing of the starting pistol sent the other runners and me chasing towards the stair slide. Apart from me, none of the elite runners seemed to have checked out the stairs. They flew wildly down the steps and struggled to cling to the handrail and pull themselves up. It took 10 floors before everyone had sorted themselves out a bit.

I used this time to calmly and effortlessly get over the slippery section of stairs as unharmed as possible. When there was grip under my feet again, I and the others could run normally at full speed.

15.2.2 Race Outfit

Light and fast—that's the ideal. If the temperatures allow it, don't cover any of the big joints. Shorts give more freedom in the knees and a top or singlet gives maximum freedom of movement in the elbows and shoulders.

In addition, the short outfits save a few grams of weight by using less fabric compared to long running clothes.

15.2.3 Energy Shot

After the starting gun and the starting line, the body runs at the limit—full speed from the very first second. To push the body and mind before the start line, I often use an energy shot. Whether from the effervescent Red Bull empire or from other nutritional supplement manufacturers like the Swiss sponsor, the content was very similar—high doses of caffeine and taurine.

It's hard to say whether it did any good, but faith alone is said to move mountains—or at least get me to the top faster.

> I could feel the effect of the energy drinks on the Park Inn Hotel during one of my starts at the SkyRun in Berlin. The start was pushed back further and further. By the time an hour had passed, I felt an almost unbearable restlessness and urge to move inside me. Surely the body's own nervousness was the main driver, but probably the shot—without the race immediately following—increased this effect noticeably. From this race onwards, I was even more attentive to the fact that the start coincided with the perceived effect as desired.

15.2.4 Compression Socks

At one time, calf socks were a must-have accessory in running. Today, a visible percentage of runners wear socks below the knee to take advantage of the compression on the calf and thus better blood circulation. At the beginning of the millennium, things were different and Paula Redcliff (ex-marathon world record holder) was one of the very few runners in the world who wore medical socks for sport. Because of my slightly thicker veins in my calves, I have been using compression stockings for every competition since the beginning of my active time; later, the manufacturer Bauerfeind became my sponsor and made it possible for me to wear customized compression socks.

At times I wore compression class two stockings. That was possible because the competitions ended after 5-10 minutes. In longer competitions, the compression would have become too strong. Besides the competition, the compression socks can be used for regeneration. More about this in the next chapter.

 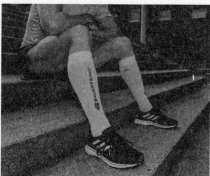

Compression socks add slight pressure to the calf.

15.2.5 Cycling Gloves

Few runners use gloves for stair running. The advantages and disadvantages are described in the chapter above and in the interview with Suzy Walsham. It is best to try what feels good and fits for you.

15.3 Regeneration

The load in stair running is high—mostly maximum. Whether in training or in competition, you feel your body and often your limits. That's why regeneration plays a very important role and is the most important parameter in performance development for professionals, apart from training. This means that if you want to be fast, you have to take care of the regeneration of your body, especially of your muscles, tendons, and mind.

15.3.1 Active Regeneration

Running loose after training and competition should be the beginning of regeneration. In this process, many waste products of the intensive metabolism under load are removed and broken down at low load.

One example of this is lactate. The salt of lactic acid builds up when not enough energy can be produced with oxygen in the muscle. The oxidation process then takes place to provide additional energy without oxygen. However, the decomposition product lactate is built up, which makes the muscle and the body feel sour. It is mainly broken down by the heart muscle, which can do this particularly well under low load.

The low load in the RECOM zone (zone 1) for some time is better than resting for faster regeneration. That is why a 5- to 10-minute run after a session will help your regeneration.

15.3.2 Alternative Sports: Swimming and Aqua Jogging

Due to the intensive load on tendons, cartilage, ligaments, and muscles, it is possible to switch to other sports for regeneration. Swimming reduces the orthopedic strain to a large extent due to the buoyancy of the water. The slightly compressive effect of the water stimulates blood circulation. This effect is enhanced by the superficial massaging effect of the water on the skin. In addition to the various swimming styles, there is the option of aqua jogging for runners. In winter, in case of injuries or overloads, this can be a very good alternative to training or support regeneration.

15.3.3 Alternative Sport: Cycling

The five-time winner of the *Empire State Building Run-Up*, Paul Crake from Australia, was a professional cyclist after his mountain running career. He has shown how useful it is for tower running to get on a bike. Because of the low orthopedic load due to the circular, fluid movement without direct contact with the ground, and because of the strong training effect on the cardiovascular system, cycling is more than a fallback solution and not just for recovery.

Cycling is like climbing stairs! If you try the motion sequence, you will easily recognize the similarity with stair climbing (i.e., the power development when the knee is in front of the body at the highest point and then goes back down). On the way down, both the pressure on the pedals and the push off the step is an almost identical movement. There are differences but the overlaps are so great that cycling is ideal for training stair running.

It's easy to notice the importance of bike training in the preparation for all my staircase running victories when you look at the training log. Dripping on the ergometer, I pedaled many hours each week during the winter months of December and January to be in top shape at the beginning of February to compete in New York at the *Empire State Building Run-Up*.

The classic endurance training consisted of 2-3 hours of easy pedaling while watching the biathlon races, triathlon world championship recording from Kona/Hawaii, etc.

To do this, I regularly tramp intervals with a look at the white wall. After a 20-minute warm-up, the dripped sweat was already in a small puddle on the floor—and then hard intervals. Starting with 250 watts for 10 minutes, the pyramid increased to 400 watts. Afterwards not only were my body and legs tired, but the puddle had become a lake.

In the summer I use the ideal conditions to ride outside. The focus is then on circumferential basic training. I can easily incorporate the intensities on the road, in the stadium, or, of course, on the stairs.

15.3.4 Stretch and Mobilize

Healthy muscle is strong and flexible!
—Thomas Dold

During exercise, parts of the muscle fibers contract and then are pulled apart again by the antagonist. The interaction works excellently and yet there are still adhesions with thousands of movements.

Exactly what happens has not yet been researched, but there is much evidence to suggest that the fascial structures surrounding each muscle play a crucial role. These thin structures, which some people have likened to white threads on a chicken thigh, run through the entire human body and surround the organs.

The loosening and release of these structures creates the increased mobility we feel after a stretching and mobilization exercise. Muscle adaptation through length growth occurs only after weeks, months, or years of appropriate training and stretching.

The stairs offer you many possibilities to stretch the most important muscle groups in an ideal way. That's why there is a separate chapter on it, so you can use these exercises for your recovery and health.

The goal is to keep your muscles, tendons, and fascia healthy, flexible, and resilient, and to keep you moving and exercising.

15.3.5 Yoga

The Sanskrit word yoga means unity and harmony. While yoga is known by many for its asanas, some of which are acrobatic gymnastic exercises, it is in essence a way of life that contains a total of eight elements, including lifestyle instructions, breathing exercises, and meditation practice.

Even when taken out of this comprehensive overall context, yoga asanas are extremely effective for exercising the body. Yogis use these exercises to increase their flexibility and physical strength, while purifying the mind.

Those who are not so spiritually inclined will still feel the beneficial effects of the exercises. Videos on this are countless online. However, if you don't have excellent body awareness per se, you should start by taking a good yoga class. With a little luck, you will find a good teacher who will help you avoid beginner mistakes and the resulting injuries.

Since 2019 I have been using yoga intensively in my own training and have done yoga teacher trainings in Ashtanga. The first exercises (primary series) are 72 defined sequences of asanas, in which both the breathing rhythm and the direction of gaze, along with the posture, are defined. Thus, you train not only the body—thereby strength, coordination, and flexibility—but also your strength to focus and maintain focus.

In the beginning it is challenging for many and the asanas are hard to do with an immobile runner's body. But this path also begins with the first step or sun salutation.

Very often in runners, the posterior thigh muscles (hamstrings) are shortened.

15.3.6 Regeneration for the Brain Through Meditation

While the body recovers for the most part from stress within 48 hours, the nervous system needs up to 72 hours. High-intensity stair running sessions, with maximum load through intervals or jumps, put an enormous strain on the nervous system.

This is noticeable through a feeling of mental fatigue and exhaustion, regardless of the physical degree of fatigue. This becomes especially clear during coordination exercises, which are physically easy, but mentally highly demanding.

But how do you regenerate the mind?

The most common method is rest: close your eyes and sleep. This works and is therefore practicable for everyone.

However, during the sleeping regeneration the load capacity of the mind does not increase; meditation, however, does that.

....

Mediation is active regeneration for the mind!
—Thomas Dold

....

Whether it is a guided meditation, looking into a candle flame, or consciously focusing on a nut in the mouth, the mind recovers and relaxes by focusing on ONE object. Sooner or later the meditators feel this themselves.

A bit more challenging at the beginning is not to use music, mantras, candles or nuts as a focus object, but your own breath. It can be difficult to feel the natural breath as it flows in and out of the nose. In that case, it is recommended to fill the runner's lungs a little more and consciously breathe more intensely. Then you can feel the breath and the feeling in the nose more easily and focus on it longer.

As with all exercises, you need patience until you notice fundamental progress. Training the mind or regenerating it with meditation is not a stair sprint.

From a yoga perspective, stair running regeneration is probably an insignificant tertiary benefit of meditation. Those who focus during the regeneration exercise will benefit from this ability the entire day and the rest of the week—every second.

Whether it's a complicated task at work or a challenging coordination exercise on the stairs, the focus you achieve through meditation is tremendous. The positive effects on life are limitless and indescribably great. Read more in chapter 19.

15.3.7 Recovery With Compression Stockings

"By wearing compression socks, marathon runners can optimize their performance during competition and positively influence muscle recovery afterwards."

—Allaert, F. A., Gardon-Mollard, C., & Benigni, J. P. (2011). Effet d'une compression élastique de classe II française (18–21 mmHg) sur l'adaptation musculaire à l'effort et la récupération des marathoniens. *Phlébologie, 64(4), 57–62.*

What is true for the high stress in a marathon is identical to my experience with the enormous stress in stair running: compression socks reduce the muscle pain in the regeneration and support it. The compression increases blood flow; the reduced pain does not stress the nervous system additionally. Whether stockings, sleeves, or complete compression clothing is the right thing to do is up to your own feeling. The same applies to the use of compression products. Whenever it doesn't feel right, you should check if the products fit properly or if you are using the right products for you.

Besides compression stockings, there are other products and options. Thigh compression sleeves relieve muscle pain after intense training and after competitions and support recovery. During a workout, they can stabilize irritated or pre-strained thigh areas.

15.3.8 Prophylaxis Tip

The ankle bandage supports and helps in the regeneration of overloads.

Those who exercise in nature or on outdoor stairs usually have to walk back down the stairs on their own. Even in buildings, there is not always the option of taking an elevator. If you are untrained, you will notice this strain in the knees and ankles at the beginning.

The ankle joints are also stressed in by the turns in buildings, especially if you run fast and sprint up the stairs.

If you have a knee or ankle support, you can check it before the first session to make sure it's working. Both joints recover faster and better with the supports due to the compression. This can be a pleasant advantage during the first sessions.

16 INTERVIEW WITH SUZY WALSHAM

The name Suzy Walsham is synonymous with tower running. In a glittering 14-year career that shows no sign of letting up, the Australian superstar has won everything there is to win.

—Towerrunning UK

Suzy wins the race up the stairs of the Eiffel Tower several times.

About Suzy Walsham

Growing up in Australia, she already laced up the spikes in her youth, winning several national titles in both the junior and open categories. With a best time of 2:01.85 min in the 800 m, she was one of the fastest Australians in middle distance and finished sixth in the 1500 m at the 2006 Commonwealth Games. A corporate career promotion saw her move to Singapore, and after many injuries and stress fractures, she started her second athletic career in the city state as a world class stair runner. Climbing buildings all over the world, she won more than 100 races, including a record 10 *Empire State Building Run-Up* wins, and became the world's most successful female stair runner.

You have won so many races around the globe; what is the race that pops up when you think of where you got most goosebumps?

I get goosebumps from many races and it's both exciting and nerve-wracking to climb a skyscraper, but my most memorable race would be *Empire State Building Run-Up*, especially my first win in 2007 and my record-breaking 10th win in 2019. Whenever people think of tower running, the first race that comes to mind is the *Empire State Building Run-Up*—it's the oldest stair climbing race and the one that is most well-known.

And which race do you think of when it comes to a very sad and disappointing one?

Also the *Empire State Building Run-Up*—in 2011. It was only five months after I had my son and I thought my fitness was okay, but I arrived in New York only the day before the race (normally I would arrive four days before) and I did not consider the impact of the 24-hour flight or the 12-hour time difference, and as I was still breastfeeding, I had to pump regularly. By the time I got to the start line, I had not slept for nearly 24 hours, I'd had to express milk throughout the night, and I was so exhausted. I was coming second or third until the last 20 floors and then I just totally lost it. I don't even remember the last ten floors and I think I ended up in fifth or sixth place and minutes off my best time. It was awful. But it also inspired me to get properly fit again and get back to racing at a high level.

The range between the highest emotions and the deepest deeps are just a few stairs and floors separated. Is this one of the things you like in tower running?

For me, I love the challenge of tower running. It's physically incredibly tough as your lactic levels go very high, yet you have to keep on pushing and climbing, so the mental strength is just as important—trying to stay focused while your body is screaming to stop. It's a very individual sport; you are competing against the building rather than other athletes. Reaching the top of a skyscraper is exhilarating.

What else makes you fly many times around the globe for the races?

I love to travel and I love big cities, so I get excited when I see new buildings and always wonder if they will have a race. I also really love to race and test and challenge myself, and as I get older it is something that I've found my body can handle better than road running. It's a really cool sport and I've met many wonderful people throughout my tower running career and seen some amazing cities.

There have been years where you won up to 17 races or were undefeated! Was that boring, exciting, or stressful?

Yes! Some years I did not have a loss which was a bit crazy. To achieve this, I would focus and concentrate on each race and just try to perform the best that I could. I was training hard all the year and I had the advantage of living in Singapore and training in different buildings, so I was able to adjust my training and the building I trained in depending on what race was coming up. The shorter races are always more difficult for me because I don't have natural speed and power; my strength was always the medium to tall buildings. It is never boring to win a race, although there were

First Place Empire State Building Run-Up.

definitely races that I won where I was not happy with my performance and thought I should have gone faster. I think this hunger to improve and perform at my best is what kept me motivated for so many years.

Men and women are normally separated in the races, but there are some time trials where everyone runs by themselves. Is that better for you compared to mixed road races?

I prefer the time trial format so then I can concentrate on my own race and finding my rhythm. For the mass starts, there is usually an elite start with only 10–15 athletes so that is manageable, as long as there is a bit of a run before reaching the stairs. Stairwells are not very wide so it can be difficult at the start and the first 10 floors for mass starts. Men and women definitely need to be separated as the guys can get a bit pushy.

There are two, three, or more times as many men running the stairs than women. What do you think women miss by not entering these races?

In a lot of sports, there is more participation by men than women. I think the challenge for tower running is that from the ages of 25 to 40 many women are busy with careers and starting families and taking time out to travel around the world for races is not easy. It's also possible that women don't know about the sport or they may think it is too hard or not enjoyable. It is an indoor sport so that might put some people off if they like doing sports outside."

On the other side, what will they gain out of running up the buildings?

There are so many health benefits from stair running. It builds strength, endurance, and power, and because of its intensity, you don't need to do a lot of it or spend hours a day training to get benefits so its great for the busy lives we all lead. For aging bodies, it also has less impact than flat running, so for anyone who gets injured a lot from running, it is the perfect sport. You also get a real high from conquering a building and that brings a sense of confidence and achievement.

In terms of training, how does female training compare to male training?

I'm not sure about the training that the men are doing, but I was training pretty hard in the stairs regularly; usually twice a week and sometimes three times a week if a big or important race was coming up. In 2012 I increased my stair training a lot and I saw a lot of improvement. It is a technical sport, and the more you can practice in a building the better you will go. In addition to stair training, I would also do road running and strength and weight training. I find that many men are better at the shorter buildings as they have the benefit of more strength and power."

Running and jumping stairs needs strength; are there specific things in training you have to take care of as a female?

I'm quite fragile as an athlete (I get injured a lot) and have had many stress fractures in the past, but I found with stair running that I had no problems with stress fractures and even with other running injuries, I would often still be able to climb the stairs with some modification to my usual technique. I would also do weighted squats and lunges in the gym to build leg strength, and as I like to use the handrail to help pull me up, I would do some arm weights as well. Also practicing in the stairs helps to build the strength that you need."

Are there different strategies in racing between men and women?

I don't think there are any different race strategies between men and women, but you always get different race strategies for different athletes (man or woman) as each athlete approaches the race differently to try for the best outcome. For me I like to get into an even pace and a good rhythm and try to maintain that to the end."

These days it's more and more that top coaches adapt the training schedule to the female cycle. Do you have experience with that and maybe some advice?

There is definitely a lot more research into the impact of the female cycle on training and competition, and I do think it is an important consideration, especially when the impacts are negative. Many women experience cramps, bloating, discomfort, heaviness, and tiredness during their cycle and their weight will also fluctuate. Each female athlete will have a different experience so it's important to consider the individual and the symptoms and experiences that they have. I was quite fortunate that I never felt adversely impacted throughout the various stages of my cycle so I didn't really have to change things up, and with so many races each year, it would be impossible to align my cycle for every race. The most important thing for a female athlete is that they are menstruating, as it's not uncommon for the stresses of training and racing to cause amenorrhea (lack of a cycle) which can have serious implications for bone health and their well-being in general.

At the Empire State Building Run-Up women run always first, and 5–10 minutes later men are racing. Did you like being the first runner in the finish compared to normal mass starts where the male winner normally crosses the finish line first?

It was amazing to be the first finisher in the race, but I think it was a big disadvantage for the men as it takes time and effort to overtake in the stairwell. A few years ago Empire State Building Run-Up changed the start format and now the elite men start first and the number of athletes is limited so a man crosses the line first and there is less traffic in the stairwell.

How do you manage being fully competitive in the races and dealing with the women you raced afterwards?

I actually found a kind of negative competitiveness when I was a track and field athlete (racing 800m and 1500m) and although many of my training environments were supporting and positive, I did have some unpleasantness at certain times when I was training with, and then competing against, some women.

Training stairs in Singapore.

I think it really depends on the individual and, similar to the corporate environment, there are going to be women that are helpful and friendly, and others that are trying to tear you down. In tower running, I've found the other women to be incredibly friendly and supportive both during races and afterwards when we are social. It's been lovely to experience, and I think we are all very encouraging of each other. We know the races are tough so we are competing against ourselves as much as each other. We are often traveling overseas to compete and its very common to go sightseeing and socializing after racing.

Is there special equipment for women running stairs?

For me, I like to use gloves to help with grip on the handrail and to stop blisters. I've been an office worker most of my professional life so the skin on my hands isn't very tough and the handrail can get sweaty and a bit slippery. I also have to tape some of my fingers as if I don't, I can get some friction blisters from pulling on the handrail and these can be really painful. I wear long compression tights for every race as it seems to help me reduce the lactic build-up and testing in training showed I was faster when wearing them. I also like to use very very light shoes with minimal support and cushioning; this helps me pivot around the stairwell easier and it feels faster. You definitely don't want a heavy, chunky shoe.

How do you manage nutrition? Are there things women have to take care of in particular?

While I don't follow a special diet and I never measure out food or count calories, I am careful about what I eat and making sure I get the nutrients I need to train hard, recover adequately, and race well. Eating enough, ensuring you have enough calcium for bone health, and keeping iron levels within the normal range is very important for female athletes. There is sometimes pressure for female athletes to be thinner and lighter, but this can be a dangerous path and result in many health problems and a decline in performance over time. My philosophy on food is that I need to be putting good things into my body to get good things out of it. I am putting my body under a lot of strain (with all the training and racing) so I need to look after it and nourish it so I can perform well.

What are your recommendations on some common injuries?

I am injured very often. When I was younger I had 14 stress fractures and a foot fracture. My last stress fracture was in 2006, and since I have been stair running, I have not had a fracture. But I still get many soft tissue injuries like muscle tears, strains, bursitis, and inflammation. Injuries can be frustrating, demotivating, and depressing, but I've learned over the years to accept the situation and try to maintain my fitness and heal as quickly as possible. I regularly see a physiotherapist and chiropractor for preventative as well as rehabilitation treatments, and I am a big believer in taking time off running (or whatever activity is causing the injury) to give the injury time to heal. Taking a week or two of no running at the beginning of the injury is better than trying to battle through, causing more damage and then needing a month off! I try to maintain my fitness as much as possible through cross training; I find I can maintain very good fitness by replicating my normal training on either an elliptical or stationary bike. For stair running, if my injury prevented me from doing a normal stair session, I would just walk the stairs to continue to use the same muscle groups and maintain some fitness (as even walking stairs raises the heart rate a bit). I also make sure I do more specific strengthening exercises to help the injury or to prevent a similar injury in the future.

Are women more sensitive in terms of feeling themselves, their body, and others? Does this affect training and racing?

I think women are more sensitive and emotional in general and can overthink things more than men. While it's still possible to block out stresses and emotions, for me I was always competing my best when I felt generally happy with my life and had less stress.

TRAINING PLANS FOR STAIR RUNNING

The plans are designed for different performance and intensity levels.

The most basic plan is for runners who want to try stair running and don't exercise that often. This plan is also suitable for game athletes who want to add stair running to their training and use the inspiration for it.

The plan for leisure runners is aimed at runners who run regularly and want to incorporate new, colorful ideas into their training. Maybe there is even a stair run nearby where a start is possible and suitable? The training plan would support the project.

If you already compete, are fit and healthy, and want to aim high, the ambitious plan is for you. Whether it's road, trail, obstacle, or tower running, the plan will help you progress and reach new experiences and possibly new performance levels with new stimuli for your body.

Disclaimer

As a coach of professional and amateur athletes, I realize that these plans will be a perfect fit for some runners, but not all. If you feel that I have written the training plan for you, then start implementing it exactly as it is. As you go along, ask yourself if this is still the case.

If you feel the plan needs some adjustment for your physique or organizational commitments, then try to understand the structure and idea behind the sessions, the sequence, and the intensities and adjust them for you.

If this description doesn't help you, think about your question and ask a good trainer you already know. If all this doesn't help, send an e-mail through my website. For every problem there is a solution.

17.1 Training Plan for Beginners and Running Enthusiasts | Once or Twice a Week

Good reasons for this training plan:

- You feel like exercising or you are full of confidence that once you start, you will get into running.
- You feel like trying something new.
- You want to experience what's in this book.
- You want to be fitter and healthier.
- You need a little more willpower in your life.
- You want to have a more defined body.
- You run because running is fun!

Requirements for This Training Plan

Motivation

Derived from the Latin movere (to move), you should have the desire to move. If you don't have it yet, your motivation often increases while you're doing it. You know this from cycling, driving, and many other examples: Overcoming the mass inertia is much more difficult than keeping the wheel in rotation. No matter how little or much you move, the training plan will bring variety.

Interest in Trying Stair Running

This training plan will almost certainly include new training elements and ideas. Therefore, it is important that you feel like trying it out and looking, feeling, and listening to yourself with the question: How do I like it?

Only those who really try out stair running will gain real experience.

Be Healthy

As with all athletic exercises, you should be healthy. A doctor can help you to clarify these issues medically, for example with a stress ECG and a large blood test. This is advisable every two years, like routine car maintenance. In addition to the medical parameters, there are other indicators of whether you feel healthy. Be honest with yourself and, if you have any doubts, postpone the start of training. Otherwise, if you're in good health, let's go or, even better, let's run!

What Will Be Your Added Value?

- You will train your willpower.
- Your body will be more trained, fitter, and more defined.
- You will feel physical limits and you will be able to push them if you want.
- You will experience new training and awaken the spirit of discovery you had as a child.
- You can infect friends and acquaintances with running fever.

Suggestions and ideas for strengthening and stretching in the training plan can be found on the pages following the training plan.

Training Plan for Beginners and Running Enthusiasts

Week 1			
Focus:	Warm up the first levels	Prerequisite: Three floors	
Monday	Start your week with walking and running; get outside for 20-30 minutes and run a few hundred yards 3-5 times.	You can recognize winners at the start. Start the day and the week actively.	Bonus session
Tuesday	Rest day		
Wednesday	Run three times for 5-10 minutes. In between, enjoy the scenery for a few minutes. After the workout, run 10 floors and take EACH step one at a time.		
Thursday	Use the day for strengthening, stretching, and coordination exercises.	Every minute is a minute for you and your body.	
Friday	Rest day		
Weekend	Warm up for 10 minutes, with walking breaks if necessary, and come to the stairs. Stretch the body for 3-5 minutes and run up the stairs 5 times. The last run should be one of the fastest, so save some energy in the first runs. Technique: 1-1 Rest: Run down slowly.	**Use a staircase with three floors.**	

Week 2			
Focus:	Continuing to warm up the first steps	**Prerequisite:** Three floors	
Monday	Start your week with walking and running; get outside for 20–30 minutes and run a few hundred yards 3–5 times.	You can recognize winners at the start. Get an active start to your day and week.	Bonus session
Tuesday	Rest day		
Wednesday	Run four times for 5–10 minutes, enjoying the scenery for a few minutes in between. Run ten flights of stairs after the workout, taking EACH step one at a time.		
Thursday	Use the day for strengthening, stretching, and coordination exercises.	Become flexible, physically and mentally.	
Friday	Rest day		
Weekend	Warm up for 10 minutes, with walking breaks if necessary, and get to the stairs. Stretch the body for 3–5 minutes and run up the stairs eight times. The last run should be one of the fastest, so save some energy in the first runs. Technique: 1-1 Rest: Run down slowly.	**Use a staircase with three floors.**	

Week 3		
Focus:	Warm up: regenerate and prepare	**Prerequisite:** No stair training
Monday	Read about running and watch YouTube videos on running technique or a running movie (e.g., No Limits about Eliud Kipchoge).	Regenerate your body and take a hot shower or bath or go for a massage.
Tuesday	Rest day	
Wednesday	Exercise for 20–30 minutes including running a few hundred meters 3–5 times. In addition, try to run backwards on a sports field on the grass three times for one minute.	Experience progress through regression.
Thursday	Use the day for strengthening, stretching, and coordination exercises.	
Friday	Rest day	
Weekend	Move for an hour; whether walking or running, the important thing is to move without a break.	

Week 4

Focus:	Stage 1: the next three levels	Prerequisite: Three floors	
Monday	Jog three times for 5–10 minutes. In between enjoy the scenery for a few minutes. Run ten floors after the workout and take EACH level one at a time.	You can recognize a winner at the start. Start the day and the week actively.	Bonus session
Tuesday	Rest day		
Wednesday	Run four times for 8–15 minutes, in between enjoy the scenery for a few minutes. Run fifteen floors after the workout and take EACH step one at a time.		
Thursday	Use the day for strengthening, stretching, and coordination exercises.	Become flexible, physically and mentally.	
Friday	Rest day		
Weekend	Warm up for 10 minutes, stretch your body for 3–5 minutes, and run up the staircase ten times. The last run should be one of the fastest, so save some energy in the first runs. In addition, try to run every other run without touching the handrail. Technique: 1-1 or 1-2 Rest: Run down slowly.	**Use a staircase with three floors.**	

Week 5

Focus:	Stage 1, Part 2: the next levels	Prerequisite: Three floors	
Monday	Jog four times for 5–10 minutes. In between, enjoy the scenery for a few minutes. Run ten flights of stairs after the workout, taking EACH step one at a time.	You can recognize a winner by their start. Start the day and the week actively	Bonus session
Tuesday	Rest day		
Wednesday	Jog four times for 8–15 minutes. In between, enjoy the scenery for a few minutes. After the workout, run 20 flights of stairs, taking EACH step one at a time.		
Thursday	Use the day for strengthening, stretching, and coordination exercises.	Become flexible, physically and mentally.	
Friday	Rest day		

(continued)

Week 5, *continued*

Weekend	Go running for 15 minutes, stretch your body for 5–8 minutes and then run up the stairs twelve times. The last run should be one of the fastest, so save some energy during the first runs. Additionally, try to touch only every second step in every second run. Technique: 1-1s or 2-2s Rest: Run down slowly.	**Use a staircase with three floors.**

Week 6

Focus:	Stage 1: regeneration and preparation	**Prerequisite:** No stair training
Monday	Read about running, watch YouTube videos on running technique.	Regenerate your body and take a hot shower or bath or go for a massage.
Tuesday	Rest day	
Wednesday	Exercise for 30–35 minutes including running a few hundred meters five times. In addition, try to run backwards on a sports field on the grass four times for one minute.	Experience progression through regression.
Thursday	Use the day for strengthening, stretching, and coordination exercises.	Become flexible, physically and mentally.
Friday	Rest day	
Weekend	Move for an hour; whether walking or running, the important thing is to move without a break.	

Week 7

Focus:	Stage 2: your ascent	**Prerequisite:** Three floors
Monday	Jog three times for 8–15 minutes. In between, enjoy the scenery for a few minutes. After the workout, run up the stairs fifteen times and take EACH step one at a time.	Winners are recognized at the start. Start the day and the week actively.
Tuesday	Rest day	
Wednesday	Run for 30–45 minutes. If you want, take a five-minute walk break in between. Run twenty flights of stairs after the workout and use the 2-1 technique (i.e., skip one step at a time on every other flight of stairs).	Change up your technique while running stairs.

Bonus session

Thursday	Change up your technique while running stairs.	
Friday	Rest day	
Weekend	Warm up for 15 minutes, stretch your body for 5–8 minutes, and then run up the stairs: 4 × in the 1-1 technique 4 × in the 2-1 technique 2 × in the 2-2 technique 1 × in the 1-1 technique Interval rest: Run down slowly Series rest: 1-2 minutes standing or mobilization exercises Cool down for 10 minutes.	**Change up your technique while running stairs.**

Week 8

Focus:	Stage 2, Part 2: your ascent	**Prerequisite:** Three floors
Monday	Run three times for 10–15 minutes, enjoying the scenery for a few minutes in between. Run fifteen flights of stairs after the workout, taking EACH step one at a time.	You can recognize winners at the start. Start the day and the week actively.
Tuesday	Rest day	
Wednesday	Run for 30–50 minute—maybe you can do it without a break? Run twenty flights of stairs after the workout and use the 2-1 technique (i.e., every second flight of stairs you skip one step at a time).	
Thursday	Use the day for strengthening, stretching, and coordination exercises.	
Friday	Rest day	
Weekend	Run for 15 minutes, stretch your body for 5–8 minutes, and then run the stairs of the three floors/comparable outdoor stairs: 3 × in the 1-1 technique 4 × in the 2-1 technique 3 × in the 2-2 technique 1 × in the 1-1 technique Interval rest: Walk down slowly. Series rest: 1–2 minutes standing or mobilization exercises Cool down for 10 minutes.	**Use a stairwell with three floors.**

Bonus session

Week 9		
Focus:	Stage 2: regeneration and preparation	**Prerequisite:** No stair training
Monday	Read about running and watch YouTube videos on running technique or a recording of a marathon.	Regenerate your body and take a hot shower or bath or go for a massage.
Tuesday	Rest day	
Wednesday	Exercise for 20–45 minutes and in between do five incremental runs where you speed up over a distance of 80 meters until you reach almost your maximum speed. In addition, integrate two intervals of 1 minutes of backward running. The break between the intervals is 1–2 minutes of slow running or walking.	Experience progression through regression.
Thursday	Use the day for strengthening, stretching, and coordination exercises.	
Friday	Rest day	
Weekend	Exercise for an hour; whether you go for a walk or a run, the important thing is to exercise without a break.	

Week 10		
Focus:	Your final	**Prerequisite:** Three floors
Monday	Move for 20–45 minutes and in between do five acceleration runs where you speed up over a distance of 80 meters, until you reach almost your maximum speed. In addition, integrate two intervals of 1 minute of backward running. The break between the intervals is 1–2 minutes of slow running or walking.	Winners are recognized at the start. Start the day and week actively. Use backward running as well. *(Bonus session)*
Tuesday	Rest day	
Wednesday	Run for 35–50 minutes. If you want, take a 5-minute walk break in between. After the workout, run twenty flights of stairs and use the 2-1 technique (i.e., skip one step at a time on every other flight of stairs).	
Thursday	Use the day for strengthening, stretching, and coordination exercises.	
Friday	Rest day	

Weekend	Run for 15 minutes, then stretch your body for 5–8 minutes, and run stairs: 2 × in the 1-1 technique 2 × in the 2-1 technique 2 × in the 2-2 technique Then do the same again for a total of twelve repetitions. Interval rest: Run down slowly. Series rest: Stand for 1–2 minutes or do mobilization exercises. Cool down for 10 minutes.	**Use a stairwell with three floors.**

Week 11

Focus:	Your final finish	**Prerequisite:** Three floors
Monday	Run for 30–60 minutes and in between do five intervals of increasing speed over a distance of 100 meters until you reach almost your maximum speed. In addition, integrate three intervals of 1 minute of backward running. The break between the intervals is 1–2 minutes of running or walking.	You can recognize winners at the start. Start the day and the week actively.
Tuesday	Rest day	
Wednesday	Run for 40–50 minutes. If you want, take a 5-minute walk break in between. After the workout, run twenty flights of stairs and use the 2-1 or 2-2 technique (i.e., skip one step at a time on every other flight of stairs).	
Thursday	Use the day for strengthening, stretching, and coordination exercises.	
Friday	Rest day	
Weekend	Run in for 15 minutes, then stretch your body for 5–8 minutes, and run stairs: 1 × in the 1-1 technique 2 × in the 2-1 technique 3 × in the 2-2 technique 1 × in the 1-1 technique with very high stride frequency Then do the same again for a total of 14 repetitions. Interval rest: Walk down slowly. Series rest: 1–2 minutes standing or mobilization exercises Run out for 10 minutes.	**Use a stairwell with three floors.**

Bonus session

Week 12		
Focus:	Your final regeneration and preparation	Prerequisite: No stair training
Monday	Read about running, or watch YouTube videos on running technique or a recording of a marathon.	Regenerate your body and take a hot shower or bath, or go for a massage.
Tuesday	Rest day	
Wednesday	Exercise for 30-60 minutes and in between do five acceleration runs where you speed up over a distance of 100 meters until you reach almost your maximum speed. Also incorporate two intervals of two minutes of running backwards. The break between intervals is 1–2 minutes of slow running or walking.	Use your reverse as well.
Thursday	Use the day for strengthening, stretching, and coordination exercises.	
Friday	Rest day	
Weekend	Exercise for an hour; whether walking or running, the important thing is to not stop.	

17.1.1 Strengthening and Stretching Exercises

Strengthening and stretching are the two sides of the same coin. Therefore, use both elements to be physically stable and flexible. Because every body, every muscle is different, there are endless possibilities and exercises for practical implementation. The following exercises are suggestions that you can adapt, modify, add to, or ignore if you train these elements, for example, in the gym or yoga classes. The page number of the exercise in the book is in parentheses.

Set 1 WARM-UP WEEKS 1–3

Warm-up: Run up 100 steps and run down 100 steps.

Rest: Recover for two minutes and stand, walk, sit, or lie down.

One round

2 × 10-second Knee Lift (p. 112)
30 seconds Stair Climber (p. 130)
60 seconds Floor Scale Plus (p. 126)

Rest: Recover for two minutes and stand, walk, or sit.

One round

Push-Up Pyramid (p. 134)
20 seconds each leg Lunge (p. 141)
20 seconds per leg Hamstrings (p. 142)
20 seconds per leg Achilles Tendon and Calf Muscles (p. 148)

Duration: 10–15 minutes

Set 2 LEVEL 1 WEEKS 4–6

Warm-up: Run up 200 steps and run down 200 steps.

Rest: Recover for two minutes and stand or walk.

Rest between rounds:
Week 4 = 2 minutes, week 5 = 1 minute, week 6 = no rest

3 × 10-second Knee Lift (p. 112)
60 seconds Stair Climber (p. 130)
60 seconds Floor Scale Plus (p. 126)

Rest: Recover for two minutes and stand or walk.

One round

Push-Up Pyramid (p. 134)
20 seconds each leg Lunge (p. 141)
2 × 20 seconds per leg Hamstrings (p. 142)
20 seconds per leg Achilles Tendon and Calf Muscles (p. 148)
30 seconds per leg Gluteal Muscles (p. 146)

Duration: 18–22 minutes

Set 3   LEVEL 2   WEEKS 7–9

Warm-up: Run up 250 steps and run down 250 steps.

Rest: Recover for two minutes and stand or walk.

Rest between rounds:
Week 7 = 2 minutes, week 8 = 1 minute, week 9 = no rest

3 × 10-second Knee Raises (p. 112)
60 seconds Stair Climber (p. 130)
60 seconds Floor Scale Plus (p. 126)

Rest: Recover for two minutes and stand or walk.

Two rounds (during week 7, rest 1–2 minutes between rounds)
Push-Up Pyramid (p. 134)
20 seconds each leg Hamstrings (p. 142)
20 seconds per leg Achilles Tendon and Calf Muscles (p. 148)
30 seconds per leg Gluteal Muscles (p. 146)

Duration: 20–25 minutes

Set 4   YOUR FINAL   WEEKS 10–12

Warm-up: Run up 250 steps and run down 250 steps.

Rest: Recover for two minutes and stand or walk.

Rest between rounds:
Week 10 = 2 minutes, week 11 = 1 minute, week 12 = no rest

3 × 10-second Knee Lift (p. 112)
60 seconds Stair Climber (p. 130)
60 seconds Floor Scale Plus (p. 126)

Rest: Recover for two minutes and stand or walk.

Two rounds (during week 10, rest 1–2 minutes between rounds)
Push-Up Pyramid (p. 134)
20 seconds each leg Lunge (p. 141)
20 seconds per leg Hamstrings (p. 142)
20 seconds per leg Achilles Tendon and Calf Muscles (p. 148)
30 seconds per leg Gluteal Muscles (p. 146)

Duration: 20–25 minutes

17.2 Training Plan for Leisure Runners | Two to Four Times a Week

Good reasons for this training plan:
- You run regularly and want variety.
- You want to give your body new stimuli.
- You want to try stair running.
- You wonder how to sprint up over 1,000 steps and why.
- You can imagine stair training supporting your goals.
- You have a desire to practice while reading the book.

Prerequisites for This Training Plan

Interest in Trying Stair Running

Stair running is different than running on the flat, and that's the great opportunity about stairs. It's a new stimulus that adds color to your everyday endurance running routine. Plus, you may get to run in new neighborhoods or buildings and on new routes.

Be Healthy

You probably value good health and notice it in your diet, sleep patterns, and alcohol consumption. It is helpful if you eat and sleep appropriately before and after stair runs. It can be that the training is more demanding than usual and then it is good to support your health and recovery. Of course you should be healthy from a medical point of view.

Injury-Free

It is helpful if you are injury-free during your first stair runs, apart from the usual niggles. The stresses on individual muscle groups can be high and if you are injury-free you reduce the risk of faulty loading and overloading.

What will be your added value?

- Your body will be trained, fitter, and more defined.
- You will train your willpower.
- Your performance will most likely increase.
- You will feel physical limits and you will be able to push them if you want.
- You will experience new training and awaken the spirit of discovery you had as a child.
- You can talk with your friends about stair running and infect them with your enthusiasm.
- You will get to know yourself and your body better.
- You will strengthen your cardiovascular and immune systems in the long term.

Suggestions and ideas for strengthening and stretching in the training plan are in the pages after the training plan.

Week 1		
Focus:	Warm up the first levels	Prerequisite: Three floors
Monday	Go for a 30-minute continuous run. Exercise, if you can, before breakfast.	You can recognize a winner by their start. Get an active start to your day and week.
Tuesday	Rest day	
Wednesday	Do a 20-minute basic endurance run. Run up 15 floors and take EACH floor one at a time. Do a 5–10-minute basic endurance run to finish.	
Thursday	Use the day for strengthening, stretching, and coordination exercises.	Every minute is a minute for you and your body.
Friday	Rest day	
Weekend	Warm up for 10 minutes, then mobilize for 5–10 minutes with stretching. Run up the stairs five times; the last run should be one of the fastest, so save some energy in the first runs. Technique: 1-1 Rest: Return slowly. Cool down for 10 minutes.	**Use a staircase with three floors.**

Bonus session

Week 2			
Focus:	Continue to warm up the first levels	**Prerequisite:** Three floors	
Monday	Go for a 30-minute basic endurance run. Exercise, if you can, before breakfast.	You can recognize a winner by their start. Start the day and the week actively.	Bonus session
Tuesday	Rest day		
Wednesday	Warm up with a 25-minute basic endurance run. Run up 15 floors and take EACH floor one at a time. Go for a 10-minute basic endurance run to finish.		
Thursday	Use the day for strengthening, stretching, and coordination exercises.	Become flexible, physically and mentally.	
Friday	Rest day		
Weekend	Warm up for 10 minutes, then mobilize for 5–10 minutes with stretching. Run up the stairs eight times. **Important:** The last run should be one of the fastest, so save some energy on the first runs. Technique: 1-1 Rest: Return slowly. Cool down for 10 minutes.	**Use a stairwell with three floors.**	

Week 3

Focus:	Regeneration and preparation	Prerequisite: No stair training
Monday	Read about running, watch YouTube videos on running technique or a running movie (e.g., No Limits about Eliud Kipchoge).	Regenerate your body and take a hot shower or bath, or go for a massage.
Tuesday	Rest day	
Wednesday	Exercise for 30–40 minutes including running visibly faster for about 400 meters 3–5 times. In addition, try to run backwards on a sports field on the grass three times for 1 minute. The break between the intervals is 1–2 minutes of loose running on the grass.	Experience progress by running backwards.
Thursday	Use the day for strengthening, stretching, and coordination exercises.	
Friday	Rest day	
Weekend	Move for one (running) or two hours (cycling) so that you can easily entertain yourself at the same time.	

Week 4

Focus:	Stage 1: the next levels	Prerequisite: Three floors	
Monday	Go for a 25-minute basic endurance run. Run up 15 floors and take EACH step one at a time. Go for a 10-minute basic endurance run to finish.	You can recognize a winner at the start. Start the day and the week actively.	Bonus session
Tuesday	Rest day		
Wednesday	Go for a 30-minute basic endurance run. Run up 6 × 3 floors, alternating each lap between the 1-1 and 2-2 techniques. Go for a 10-minute basic endurance run to finish.		
Thursday	Use the day for strengthening, stretching, and coordination exercises.		
Friday	Rest day		

Weekend	Warm up for 10 minutes, then mobilize for 5–10 minutes with stretching. Run up the staircase 10 times. **Important:** The last run should be one of the fastest, so save some energy on the first runs. Technique: 1-1 Rest: Return slowly. Cool down for 10 minutes.	**Use a stairwell with three floors.**

Week 5

Focus:	Stage 1, Part 2: the next levels	**Prerequisite:** Five floors
Monday	Go for a 30-minute basic endurance run. Run up 15 floors and take EACH level individually. Go for a 10-minute basic endurance run to finish.	You can recognize a winner at the start. Start the day and the week actively. *Bonus session*
Tuesday	Rest day	
Wednesday	Go for a 30-minute basic endurance run. Do three coordination and three strengthening exercises. Run up 6 × 3 floors, alternating each round between the 1-1 and 2-2 techniques. Go for a 10-minute basic endurance run to wind down.	
Thursday	Use the day for strengthening, stretching, and coordination exercises.	
Friday	Rest day	
Weekend	Warm up for 10 minutes, then mobilize for 5–10 minutes with stretching. Run up 3 × 4 floors, alternating each round between the 1-1 and 2-2 techniques. **Important:** The last run should be one of the fastest, so save some energy on the first runs. Interval rest: Return slowly. Series rest: Stand for 1–2 minutes or do mobilization exercises. Cool down for 10 minutes.	**Use a stairwell with three floors.**

Week 6

Focus:	Stage 1: regeneration and preparation	Prerequisite: No stair training
Monday	Read about running, watch YouTube videos on running technique.	Regenerate your body and take a hot shower or bath, or go for a massage.
Tuesday	Rest day	
Wednesday	Do 30–40 minutes of exercise including running visibly faster 5 × 400 meters. In addition, try to run backwards on a sports field on the grass for 4 × 1 minute. The break between the intervals is 1–2 minutes of easy running.	Experience progress by running backwards.
Thursday	Use the day for strengthening, stretching, and coordination exercises.	Become flexible, physically and mentally.
Friday	Rest day	
Weekend	Move around for one (running) or two hours (cycling) in such a way that you can easily entertain yourself at the same time.	**Use a staircase with five floors.**

Week 7

Focus:	Stage 2: your ascent	Prerequisite: Five floors	
Monday	Go for a 30-minute basic endurance run. Run up 15 floors using the 1-1 technique; include five coordination exercises over two floors each. Go for a 10-minute basic endurance run to finish.	Winners are recognized at the start. Start the day and the week actively.	Bonus session
Tuesday	Rest day		
Wednesday	Go for a 30-minute basic endurance run. Do three coordination and three strengthening exercises. Run up 8 × 3 floors, alternating each round between the 1-1 and 2-2 techniques. Do a 10-minute basic endurance run to cool down.	Note: You can also try a change of technique while running up and down stairs.	
Thursday	Use the day for strengthening, stretching, and coordination exercises.		
Friday	Rest day		

| Weekend | Warm up for 15 minutes; mobilize for 5–10 minutes with stretching. After that:
1× in the 1-1 technique
3× in the 2-1 technique
3× in the 2-2 technique
1× in the 1-1 technique
Interval rest: Run down slowly.
Series rest: Stand or do mobilization exercises for 1–2 minutes.
Cool down for 10 minutes. | **Use a staircase with five floors.** |

Week 8

Focus:	Stage 2, Part 2: your ascent	**Prerequisite:** Five floors
Monday	Go for a 30-minute basic endurance run. Run up 15 floors, using the 1-1 technique; include five coordination exercises over two floors each. Go for a 10-minute basic endurance run to finish.	Winners are recognized at the start. Start the day and the week actively.
Tuesday	Rest day	
Wednesday	Go for a 30-minute basic endurance run. Do three coordination and three strengthening exercises. Run up 10 × 3 floors, alternating each round between 1-1, 2-1, and 2-2 techniques. Go for a 10-minute basic endurance run to wind down.	
Thursday	Use the day for strengthening, stretching, and coordination exercises.	
Friday	Rest day	
Weekend	Warm up for 15 minutes; mobilize for 5–10 minutes mobilization with stretching. After that: 2× in the 1-1 technique 3× in the 2-1 technique 4× in the 2-2 technique 1× in the 1-1 technique Interval rest: Return slowly. Series rest: Stand or do mobilization exercises for 1–2 minutes. Cool down for 10 minutes.	**Use a staircase with five floors.**

Bonus session

Week 9

Focus:	Stage 2: regeneration and preparation	Prerequisite: No stair training
Monday	Read about running, watch YouTube videos on running technique or a recording of a marathon.	Regenerate your body and take a hot shower or bath, or go for a massage.
Tuesday	Rest day	
Wednesday	Go for a 45-minute basic endurance run, and do five acceleration runs where you speed up over a distance of 100 meters until you reach almost your maximum speed. Also include 4 × 1 minute backward running. The break between the intervals is 1–2 minutes of easy forward running.	Experience progression through regression.
Thursday	Use the day for strengthening, stretching, and coordination exercises.	
Friday	Rest day	
Weekend	Move for one (running) or two hours (cycling) at a pace that allows you to easily talk to yourself.	

Week 10

Focus:	Your final	Prerequisite: Five floors	
Monday	Go for a 30-minute basic endurance run. Run up15 floors, using the 1-1 technique; include five coordination exercises over three floors each. Go for a 10-minute basic endurance run to finish.	Winners are recognized at the start. Start the day and the week actively.	Bonus session
Tuesday	Rest day		
Wednesday	Go for a 30-minute basic endurance run. Do three coordination and three strengthening exercises. Run up 10 × 3 floors, alternating each round between the 1-1, 2-1, and 2-2 techniques. Do every third run really fast. Go for a 10-minute basic endurance run to finish.		
Thursday	Use the day for strengthening, stretching, and coordination exercises.		
Friday	Rest day		

| Weekend | Warm up for 15 minutes; mobilize for 5–10 minutes with stretching. After that: 2× in the 1-1 technique, 1× of it very fast 3× in the 2-1 technique, 1× of it very fast 4× in the 2-2 technique, 1× of it very fast 1× in the 1-1 technique Interval rest: Return slowly. Series rest: Stand or do mobilization exercises for 2 minutes. Cool down for 10 minutes. | **Use a stairwell with five floors.** |

Week 11

Focus:	Your final finish	**Prerequisite:** 200 steps | > 10 floors	
Monday	Go for a 30-minute basic endurance run. Run up 15 floors, using the 1-1 technique; include five coordination exercises over three floors each. Go for a 10-minute basic endurance run to finish.	Winners are recognized at the start. Start the day and the week actively.	Bonus session
Tuesday	Rest day		
Wednesday	Go for a 30-minute basic endurance run. Do three coordination and three strengthening exercises. Run up 10 × 3 floors and alternate each round between 1-1, 2-1, and 2-2; do every other run really fast. Go for a 10-minute basic endurance run to cool down.		
Thursday	Use the day for strengthening, stretching, and coordination exercises.		
Friday	Rest day		
Weekend	Warm up for 15 minutes; mobilize for 5–10 minutes with stretching. Climb 200 steps (e.g., in the vineyard) or > 10 floors: 1 × medium intensity, 1-1 technique 1 × MAXIMAL (with 1 minute break at half time!) 1 × MAXIMUM Interval rest: Return slowly. Series rest: Stand, run easy, or do mobilization exercises for 3 minutes. Cool down for 10 minutes.	**Use > 10 floors or a natural staircase with at least 200 steps.**	

Week 12		
Focus:	Your final regeneration and preparation	**Prerequisite:** No stair training
Monday	Go for a 30-minute basic endurance run. Run up 15 floors, using the 1-1 technique; include five coordination exercises over three floors each. Go for a 10-minute basic endurance run to finish.	Regenerate your body and take a hot shower or bath, or go for a massage.
Tuesday	Rest day	
Wednesday	Do 60 minutes of basic endurance running in between 8 incline runs where you speed up over a distance of 100 meters until you reach almost your maximum speed. Also integrate 3 × 2 minutes of backward running. The break between the intervals is 1–2 minutes of easy running.	Also use your backward gear.
Thursday	Use the day for strengthening, stretching, and coordination exercises.	
Friday	Rest day	
Weekend	Move for one (running) or two to three hours (cycling) in such a way that you can easily talk as you exercise.	

17.2.1 Strengthening and Stretching Exercises

Strengthening and stretching are two sides of the same coin. Therefore, use both elements to be physically stable and flexible. Because every body, every muscle is different, there are endless possibilities and exercises of practical implementation. The following exercises are a suggestion that you can adapt, modify, add to or ignore—for example, when training these elements in the gym or yoga classes. Depending on your abilities, one round on the stairs ideally includes 20-40 steps.

Set 1   WARM-UP   WEEKS 1-3

Warm-up: Run up 200 steps and run down 200 steps.

Rest: Recover for 1-2 minutes and stand, walk, sit, or lie down.

One round

Two rounds of Knee Lift (p. 112).
30 seconds Stair Climber (p. 130)
60 seconds Standing Balance Plus (p. 126)

Rest: Recover for two minutes and stand, walk, or sit.

Two rounds

Push-Up Pyramid (p. 134)
20 seconds each leg Lunge (p. 141)
20 seconds per leg Hamstrings (p. 142)
20 seconds per leg Achilles Tendon and Calf Muscles (p. 148)

Duration: 15-20 minutes

Set 2   LEVEL 1   WEEKS 4–6

Warm-up: Run up 250 steps and run down 250 steps.

Rest: Recover for 1–2 minutes and stand or walk.

Two rounds
2 × rounds of Knee Lift (p. 112)
30 seconds Stair Climber (p. 130)
60 seconds Floor Scale Plus (p. 126)

Rest: Recover for two minutes and stand or walk.

Two rounds
Push-Up Pyramid (p. 134)
20 seconds each leg Lunge (p. 141)
20 seconds per leg Hamstrings (p. 142)
20 seconds per leg Achilles Tendon and Calf Muscles (p. 148)

Duration: 18–22 minutes

Set 3   LEVEL 2   WEEKS 7–9

Warm-Up: Run up 250 steps and run down 250 steps.

Rest: Recover for 1–2 minutes and stand or walk.

One round

Two rounds of Double Skipping (p. 113)
• Two rounds of down Shaolin Walk (p. 132)
Two rounds of as many steps as possible
• Two rounds of down Step–Sit (p. 128)
30 second Stair Climber (p. 130)

Rest: Recover for two minutes and stand or walk.

Two rounds
Push-Up Pyramid (p. 134)
20 seconds each leg Lunge (p. 141)
20 seconds per leg Posterior Hamstrings (p. 142)
20 seconds per leg Adductors (p. 144)
20 seconds per leg Achilles Tendon and Calf Muscles (p. 148)

Duration: 18–22 minutes

Set 4   YOUR FINAL   WEEKS 10–12

Warm-Up: Run up 300 steps and run down 300 steps.

Rest: Recover 1–2 minutes and stand or walk.

One round

Two rounds of Double Skipping (p. 113).
• Two rounds of down Shaolin Walk (p. 132).
Two rounds of as many steps as possible
• Two rounds of down Step–Sit (p. 128)
30 second Stair Climber (p. 130)

Rest: Recover for two minutes and stand or walk.

Two rounds

Push-Up Pyramid (p. 134)
20 seconds each leg Lunge (p. 141)
20 seconds per leg Hamstrings (p. 142)
20 seconds per leg Achilles Tendon and Calf Muscles (p. 148)
30 seconds per leg Gluteal Muscles (p. 146)

Duration: 20–25 minutes

17.3 Training Plan for Ambitious Athletes | Four+ Times per Week

Good reasons for this training plan:

- You want to be able to run faster.
- You know about running and want to try new things.
- You have heard about stair running and want to try it.
- You like to push boundaries.
- You love to have your pulse pounding and thighs burning every now and then.

Prerequisites for This Workout Plan

Interest in Trying Stair Running

You run regularly and love it. At the same time, you need new stimuli and you specifically incorporate them into your training. So why not try out stair running and then use it as a permanent training element?

Be Healthy

You know how to help your body prepare for training and recover afterwards. Everything that applies to normal flat running is also valid in stair running and maybe even more relevant.

From a medical perspective, you should be healthy for training.

Injury-Free

Be as injury-free as possible to bring your potential to the steps. If you start with bad posture, you usually miss your chance. The stresses on individual muscle groups (e.g., from running curves) can be high. If you're injury-free, you reduce the risk of misuse and overuse.

What will be your added value?

- You will train your willpower for other competitions.
- Your performance will most likely increase.
- You will be able to push physical limits.
- You will increase your coordination through new exercises.
- You will get to know yourself and your body better.
- You may even get to know yourself better in a new training environment and under maximum stress.
- You increase your bounce and strength endurance.

Suggestions and ideas for strengthening and stretching will follow the training plan.

Week 1

Focus:	Warming up the first levels	Prerequisite: Three floors
Monday	Run continuously for 45 minutes. Exercise, if you can, before breakfast.	You can recognize winners at the start. Have an active start to the day and week.
Tuesday	Rest day	
Wednesday	Go for a 25-minute basic endurance run. Run up 20 stories and take EACH step one at a time. Go for a 5–10-minute basic endurance run to finish.	
Thursday	Use the day for strengthening, stretching, and coordination exercises.	Every minute is a minute for you and your body.
Friday	Rest day	
Weekend	Warm up for 15 minutes, then do 5–10 minutes of mobilization with stretching. Run up the staircase 8 times. The last run should be one of the fastest, so save some energy on the first runs. Technique: 1-1 Rest: Return slowly. Cool down for 10 minutes.	**Use a stairwell with three floors.**

Week 2

Focus:	Continuing to warm up the first steps	Prerequisite: Five floors
Monday	Run for 45 continuous minutes. Exercise, if you can, before breakfast.	You can recognize winners when they start. Get an active start to the day and week.
Tuesday	Rest day	
Wednesday	Go for a 30-minute basic endurance run. Run up 25 stories and alternate between the 1-1 and 2-2 techniques each round. Go for a 5–10-minute basic endurance run to wind down.	
Thursday	Use the day for strengthening, stretching, and coordination exercises.	Become flexible, physically and mentally.
Friday	Rest day	
Weekend	Warm up for 15 minutes, then do 5–10 minutes of mobilization with stretching. Run up the stairs 7 times. The last run should be one of the fastest. Technique: 1-1 and 2-2 Rest: Return slowly. Cool down for 10 minutes.	**Use a stairwell with five floors.**

Week 3

Focus:	Regeneration and preparation	Prerequisite: No stair training
Monday	Go for a 45-minute basic endurance run for active recovery. Train before breakfast if you can.	
Tuesday	Read about running, watch YouTube videos on running technique or a running movie (e.g., No Limits about Eliud Kipchoge).	Regenerate your body and take a hot shower or bath, or go for a massage.
Wednesday	Do 50 minutes of continuous running including visibly faster about 400 meters 5 times. In addition, try to run three times for one minute backwards on a sports field on the grass. The break between the intervals is one minute of easy forward running.	Experience progress by running backwards.
Thursday	Use the day for strengthening, stretching, and coordination exercises.	
Friday	Rest day	
Weekend	Do 70 minutes of a basic endurance run or 120 minutes of cycling at very low intensity; you should be able to talk easily.	

Week 4

Focus:	Stage 1: the next levels	Prerequisite: Five floors
Monday	Go for a 45-minute basic endurance run. Exercise, if you can, before breakfast.	You can recognize winners when they start. Get an active start to your day and week.
Tuesday	Rest day	
Wednesday	Do a 30-minute basic endurance run. Run up 25 stories and alternate each lap between the 1-1 and 2-2 techniques. Do a 5-10-minute basic endurance run to wind down.	
Thursday	Use the day for strengthening, stretching, and coordination exercises.	
Friday	Go for a 60-minute basic endurance run; include five acceleration runs up to 90 percent of your max speed; rest in between for more than one minute.	

Weekend	Warm up for 15 minutes, then do 5–10 minutes of mobilization with stretching. Run up the staircase eight times. The last run should be one of the fastest. Technique: 1-1 and, if possible, 2-2 Rest: Return slowly. Cool down for 10 minutes.	**Use a stairwell with five floors.**

Week 5

Focus:	Stage 1, Part 2: the next levels	**Prerequisite:** Five floors
Monday	Go for a 45-minute basic endurance run. Run up 15 floors using the 1-1 technique with as high a frequency as possible. Train, if you can, before breakfast.	You can recognize a winner at the start. Start the day and the week actively.
Tuesday	Rest day	
Wednesday	Go for a 30-minute basic endurance run. Run up 30 stories and alternate between the 1-1 and 2-2 techniques each round. Go for a 5–10-minute basic endurance run to wind down.	
Thursday	Use the day for strengthening, stretching, and coordination exercises. Become flexible, physically and mentally.	
Friday	Do a 60-minute basic endurance run; include five incline runs up to 90 percent of your max speed; rest in between for more than one minute.	
Weekend	Warm up for 15 minutes, do 5–10 minutes of mobilization with stretching. After that: 2× in the 1-1 technique very fast 3× in the 2-1 technique, 1× of it very fast 4× in the 2-2 technique, 2× of it very fast 1× in the 1-1 technique Interval rest: Return slowly. Series rest: Two minutes of standing or mobilization exercises Cool down for 10 minutes.	**Use a stairwell with five floors.**

Week 6		
Focus:	Stage 1: regeneration and preparation	**Prerequisite:** No stair running
Monday	Do 50 minutes of basic endurance running for active recovery. Exercise before breakfast if you can.	
Tuesday	Read about running, watch YouTube videos on running technique or a running movie (e.g., No Limits about Eliud Kipchoge).	Regenerate your body and take a hot shower or bath, or go for a massage.
Wednesday	Do 50 minutes of basic endurance running including running visibly faster about 400 meters 5 times. In addition, try to run backwards on a sports field on the grass four times for 1 minute each. The break between the intervals is one minute of loose running on the grass.	Experience progress by running backwards.
Thursday	Use the day for strengthening, stretching, and coordination exercises.	Become flexible, physically and mentally.
Friday	Rest day	
Weekend	Do 80 minutes of basic endurance running or 150 minutes of cycling at very low intensity; you should be able to talk easily.	

Week 7		
Focus:	Stage 2: your ascent	**Prerequisite:** Five floors
Monday	Go for a 45-minute basic endurance run. Run up 15 floors using the 1-1 technique with as high a frequency as possible. Do five coordination exercises over two floors each.	Winners are recognized at the start. Start the day and the week actively.
Tuesday	Rest day	
Wednesday	Go for a 30-minute basic endurance run. Run up 30 flights of stairs; include 5× two flights of stairs jumps. Go for a 5-10-minute basic endurance run to finish.	Change your technique while running stairs.
Thursday	Use the day for strengthening, stretching, and coordination exercises.	
Friday	Do a 60-minute basic endurance run; include six acceleration runs up to 90 percent of your max speed. Rest in between for over one minute.	

| Weekend | Weekend
Warm up for 15 minutes, mobilize for 5–10 minutes with stretching. After that:
2× in the 1-1 technique very fast
3× in the 2-1 technique, 1× of it very fast
5× in the 2-2 technique, 3× of it very fast
1× in the 1-1 technique
Interval rest: Return slowly.
Series rest: 1–2 minutes of standing or mobilization exercises
Cool down for 10 minutes. | Use a stairwell with five floors. |

Week 8

Focus:	Stage 2: your climb continues	Prerequisite: Five floors
Monday	Go for a 45-minute basic endurance run. Run up 20 floors using the 1-1 technique with as high a frequency as possible. Do five coordination exercises over two floors each.	Winners are recognized at the start. Start the day and the week actively.
Tuesday	Rest day	
Wednesday	Go for a 30-minute basic endurance run. Run up 30 floors; include 2–3 floors of stair jumps five times. Go for a 5–10-minute basic endurance run to finish.	Change your technique for stair running.
Thursday	Use the day for strengthening, stretching, and coordination exercises.	
Friday	Go for a 60-minute basic endurance run; include six acceleration runs up to 90 percent of your max speed; rest in between for at least one minute.	
Weekend	Warm up for 15 minutes, do 5–10 minutes of mobilization with stretching. After that: 2× in the 1-1 technique very fast 3× in the 2-1 technique, 1× of it very fast 5× in the 2-2 technique, 3× of it very fast 1× in the 1-1 technique Interval rest: Return slowly. Series rest: Stand or do mobilization exercises for one minute. Cool down for 10 minutes.	Use a staircase with five floors.

Week 9

Focus:	Stage 2: regeneration and preparation	Prerequisite: No stair running
Monday	Go for a 50-minute basic endurance run for active recovery. Exercise before breakfast if you can.	
Tuesday	Read about running or watch YouTube videos on running technique or a recording of a marathon.	Regenerate your body and take a hot shower or bath, or go for a massage.
Wednesday	Do 50 minutes of basic endurance running including 5 times of running about 400 meters visibly faster. In addition, try to run 4 × 1 minute backwards on a sports field on the grass. The break between the intervals is one minute of easy running.	Experience progression through regression.
Thursday	Use the day for strengthening, stretching, and coordination exercises.	Become flexible, physically and mentally.
Friday	Rest day	
Weekend	Go for 80 minutes of basic endurance running or 150 minutes of cycling at a very low intensity; you should be able to talk easily.	

Week 10

Focus:	Your final	300 steps | > 15 floors
Monday	Do 45 minutes of basic endurance running. Run up 20 floors using the 1-1 technique with as high a frequency as possible. Do five coordination exercises over two floors each.	Winners are recognized at the start. Start the day and the week actively.
Tuesday	Rest day	
Wednesday	Go for a 30-minute basic endurance run. Run up 30 floors; include 2-3 floors of stair jumps five times. Do 5-10 minutes of basic endurance running to cool down.	Change your technique for stair running.
Thursday	Use the day for strengthening, stretching, and coordination exercises.	
Friday	Go for a 60-minute basic endurance run; include six acceleration runs up to 90 percent of your max speed; rest in between for at least one minute.	

| Weekend | Warm up for 15 minutes, do 5–10 minutes of mobilization with stretching. Run up 300 steps (e.g., in a vineyard) or more than 15 floors.
1× 80% maximum, start slow and get faster, using the 1-2 and 2-2 techniques
1× medium/high intensity, using the 1-1 technique
1× MAXIMUM
Interval rest: Run down slowly.
Series rest: Stand, jog, or do mobilization exercises for 3 minutes.
Cool down for 10 minutes. | **Use more than 15 floors or a natural staircase with at least 300 steps.** |

Week 11

Focus:	Your final finish	300 steps | > 15 floors
Monday	Do 45 minutes of basic endurance running. Run up 20 floors using the 1-1 technique with as high a frequency as possible. Do five coordination exercises over two floors each.	Winners are recognized at the start. Start the day and the week actively.
Tuesday	Rest day	
Wednesday	Do 30 minutes of basic endurance running. Run up 30 floors – include 2-3 floors of stair jumps five times. Do 5–10 minutes of basic endurance running to cool down.	Try changing your technique for stair running.
Thursday	Use the day for strengthening, stretching, and coordination exercises.	
Friday	Do 60 minutes of basic endurance running; include six hill climbs up to 90 percent of your max speed. Rest in between for at least one minute.	
Weekend	Warm up for 15 minutes; do 5–10 minutes of mobilization with stretching. Run up 300 steps (e.g., in a vineyard) or at least 15 floors. 1× 80% maximum, start slow and get faster, using the 1-2, 2-2 technique 1× MAXIMUM with a 1-minute break at half time! 1× medium/high intensity, using the 1-1 technique 1× MAXIMUM with a 1-minute break at half time! 1× MAXIMUM Interval rest: Return slowly. Series rest: Stand, jog, or do mobilization exercises for 3 minutes. Cool down for 10 minutes.	**Use at least 15 floors or a natural staircase with at least 300 steps.**

Week 12		
Focus:	Your final regeneration and preparation	**Prerequisite:** No stair training
Monday	Do 50 minutes of basic endurance running for active recovery. Training, if you can, should be before breakfast.	
Tuesday	Read about running or watch YouTube videos on running technique or a recording of a marathon.	Regenerate your body and take a hot shower or bath, or go for a massage.
Wednesday	Do 60 minutes of basic endurance running including five intervals of running visibly faster for about 400 meters. In addition, try to run backwards on a sports field on the grass for four 1-minute intervals. The break between the intervals is one minute of easy forward running.	Experience progression through regression.
Thursday	Use the day for strengthening, stretching, and coordination exercises.	
Friday	Rest day	
Weekend	Do 90 minutes of basic endurance running or 180 minutes of very low intensity cycling; you should be able to talk easily.	

17.3.1 Strengthening and Stretching Exercises

Strengthening and stretching are the two sides of the same coin. Therefore, use both elements to be physically stable and flexible. Because every body, every muscle is different, there are endless possibilities and exercises of practical implementation.

The following exercises are a suggestion that you can adapt, modify, add to, or ignore for yourself if you train these elements in the gym or in yoga classes, for example. Depending on your capabilities, one round on the stairs ideally includes 30-50 steps.

Set 1   WARM-UP   WEEKS 1-3

Warm-up: Run up 400 steps and run down 400 steps.

Rest: Recover for 1-2 minutes and stand, walk, sit, or lie down.

One round

2 rounds of Knee Lift (p. 112)
30 seconds of Stair Climber (p. 130)
60 seconds Floor Scale Plus (p. 126)

Rest: Recover for 1-2 minutes and stand, walk, or sit.

Two rounds

Push-Up Pyramid (p. 134)
20 seconds each leg Lunge (p 141)
20 seconds per leg Posterior Hamstrings (p. 142)
20 seconds per leg Adductors (p. 144)
20 seconds per leg Glutes (p. 146)
20 seconds per leg Achilles Tendon and Calf Muscles (p. 148)

Duration: 20-25 minutes

Set 2   STAGE 1   WEEKS 4–6

Warm-up: Run up 500 steps and run down 500 steps.

Rest: Stand or walk for one minute.

One round

2 rounds of Knee Lift (p. 112).
30 seconds of Stair Climber (p. 130)
60 seconds Floor Scale Plus (p. 126)

Rest: Recover for 1–2 minutes and stand, walk, or sit.

Two rounds

Push-Up Pyramid (p. 134)
20 seconds each leg Lunge (p. 141)
20 seconds per leg Posterior Hamstrings (p. 142)
20 seconds per leg Adductors (p. 144)
20 seconds per leg Glutes (p. 146)
20 seconds per leg Achilles Tendon and Calf Muscles (p. 148)

Duration: 20–25 minutes

Set 3   STAGE 2   WEEKS 7–9

Warm-up: Run up 500 steps and run down 500 steps.

Rest: Stand or walk for one minute to recover.

One round

Two rounds of Double Skipping (p. 113)
• Two rounds of down Shaolin Walk (p. 132)
Two rounds of as many steps as possible
• Two rounds of down Step-Sit (p. 128)
30 second Stair Climber (p. 130)

Rest: Recover for 1–2 minutes and stand, walk, or sit.

Two rounds

Push-Up Pyramid (p. 134)
20 seconds per leg Lunge (p. 141)
20 seconds per leg Hamstrings (p. 142)
20 seconds per leg Adductors (p. 144)
20 seconds per leg Glutes (p. 146)
20 seconds per leg Achilles Tendon and Calf Muscles (p. 148)

Duration: 20-25 minutes

Set 4   YOUR FINAL   WEEKS 10–12

Warm-up: Run up 500 steps and run down 500 steps.

Rest: Stand or walk for one minute to recover.

Two rounds

Two rounds of Double Skipping (p. 113)
• Two rounds of down Shaolin Walk (p. 132)
Two rounds of as many steps as possible
• Two rounds of down Step–Sit (p. 128)
30 second Stair Climber (p. 130)

Rest: Recover for 1–2 minutes and stand, walk, or sit.

Two rounds

Push-Up Pyramid (p. 134)
20 seconds each leg Lunge (p. 141)
20 seconds per leg Posterior Hamstrings (p. 142)
20 seconds per leg Adductors (p. 144)
20 seconds per leg Glutes (p. 146)
20 seconds per leg Achilles Tendon and Calf Muscles (p. 148)

Duration: 25-30 minutes

TOWER RUNNING MAJORS

18.1 International

18.1.1 Empire State Building Run-Up (ESB Run-Up) | USA

The Wimbledon of Tower Running

Since 1978, the run-up to the world-famous New York landmark has been an annual event. The resounding sound of the foghorn in the lobby of one of the world's tallest buildings sends runners on their journey up 320 meters of stairs—1,576 steps—to the Observation Deck on the 86th floor and open air with a view over a world metropolis and running participants sprinting the last 80 meters flat towards the finish.

Two changes of staircases and an associated change in the staircase structure make the run technically varied and challenging. The mass start is full of adrenaline which is characteristic for this race. Beginning in 2012 the start time was moved from 10:35 in the morning to 20:00 in the evening. At the same time, only 20–30 elite athletes are sent into the race together. The number of participants increased from about 300 to 800, as the non-elite participants start individually with chip timing in the stairwell. Among men, Thomas Dold holds the record for the most victories with a total of seven achieved between 2006 and 2012; among women, Suzy Walsham holds the record with ten wins between 2007 and 2019. For more information, visit

www.esbnyc.com/empire-state-building-run

18.1.2 Taipei 101 | Taiwan

The world's tallest building from 2004 to 2009 offers stair-running fun over 91 floors, 390 vertical meters, and 2,046 steps. The staircase is painted gray, and has a green handrail and neon floor indicators on each landing, so there is nothing to distract from the ascent to the Asian sky.

The last five colorfully painted floors prepare you for the brilliant view over the mega-city. The view is uninterrupted by other buildings. With 5,000 starters, the race, which has been held since 2005, is an opportunity for the public to experience their landmark physically and with their feet on this day. All participants start with a chip, so that it is only clear at the finish line which place has been achieved.

18.1.3 Sydney Tower Run-Up | Australia

The tower run-up in the Olympic city has been held since 1990. The first meters lead through the building in a somewhat complicated way, and then up the 1,504 steps in the narrow stairwell. You have to be a little careful when grabbing the handrail: If you grab it too hard and touch the wall, you risk scratching your fingertips on the craggy plaster. However, you can almost guarantee that you won't feel any pain on your fingers until you reach the finish line—the staircase demands everything.

18.1.4 Swissotel Vertical Marathon | Singapore

The 226-meter-high hotel impresses after 1,336 steps and 73 floors with a breathtaking finish on the helipad. Free of any fences, the view can sweep unhindered over the city-state. The stairwell is pleasantly tempered by the air-conditioned rooms despite the tropical heat outside. On the last five floors, the tropical heat comes down to the runners through the open door for an added challenge.

18.1.5 Niesen Stair Run | Switzerland

Runners must overcome 11,674 steps and 1,669 meters of altitude difference on the stairs next to the mountain railway on the Swiss mountain Niesen (2,362 meters high), the longest stair run in the world. The record time of 55:55:70 minutes is held by Emmanuel Vaudan. For more information, visit

www.niesen.ch/en/stairway-run/

18.2 Germany

18.2.1 Sky-Run Berlin

One of the highest viewing platforms in Berlin awaits you after 770 steps and 128 meters of altitude, spread over 39 floors. The running event at Alexanderplatz is now popular throughout Europe with firefighters, who race through the stairwell in full protective gear.

18.2.2 Frankfurt Trade Fair Tower

With 61 floors, 1,200 steps, and 222 meters of elevation, the run to the top of Frankfurt's skyscraper is a challenge for national and international runners. The stairwell is laid out in a triangular plan, with the longest side being flat and the two short sides each being the step areas. This allows for a short breather on each floor, at least for a few meters.

18.2.3 TK Tower-Run Rottweil

The test tower for ropeless multidirectional elevators also needs an escape stairwell and this opens the doors for the 1,320-step climb every year. On the viewing platform at a height of 232 meters, you can see forests and nature instead of canyons of houses. For more information, visit

https://towerrun.tkelevator.com/infos_en/

18.2.4 Mt. Everest Stair Marathon

If you want to climb Mt. Everest in Germany, Radebeul near Dresden is the place to go. The 100 rounds on the Spitzhausen stairs up and down through the vineyards mean 8,848 meters of altitude up and down and a double marathon (84.4 kilometers)— a very special ultramarathon. The fastest to complete the task were Andreas Allwang in 13:26:53 hours and Antje Müller in 16:16:56 hours. For more information, visit

www.treppenmarathon.de

18.3 Tower-Running Directory

18.3.1 Towerrunning.com

The website of the Austrian founder Michael Reichetzeder has been the portal for everyone who is interested in tower running for more than 25 years. You can easily and quickly find a suitable run in your area or even far away on another continent. With details such as steps, floors, and altitude in meters, you immediately get a first impression of what to expect on site. The platform lists hundreds of stair runs around the world. For more information, visit

www.towerrunning.com

18.3.2 Vertical World Circuit

The Vertical World Circuit combines some of the most important and highest towerruns in the world into one series. The top stars of the scene are invited to the races and ensure top class in these competitions. In addition, because of the high standards of organization, these races also offer a competitive travel destination for less ambitious runners. Information about the races is available online at

www.verticalworldcircuit.com

19 FOCUS AND MENTAL TRAINING

In addition to physical training, there has been a growing tendency in recent years to train the mind as well. Either to get better or to ensure that the athlete performs at his or her best in competition. The reasons for the interest in focus and mental training are as diverse as the causes. You might wonder:

- Why didn't athletes need mental training 50 years ago to perform at their best?

- In some sports, is it the few seconds that you run faster or the centimeters that you go higher or farther that make up mental training, among other things?

Fifty years ago there was no Internet, no cell phone, and no low-cost airlines. The world of personal action and interests was smaller and there were fewer options in almost all areas. Today, the opposite is everyday life. Multi-optional and in every area—in the supermarket, in clothing, travel, sports, jobs, and vacation destinations. The consumer industry omnipresently gives you the feeling that something will be missed if you don't use the respective product. In addition, there is peer pressure in society that reinforces this effect; who wants to feel like an outsider?

Today athletes, regardless of performance level, engage in mental training to avoid experiencing these issues.

19.1 Focus on Stair Running and on Life

The benefits of focusing, which in everyday life is often equivalent to concentrating, are immense and the basis for success.

Concentrating involves keeping your attention on a single point—preferably an activity or object. As soon as the concentration decreases, you try to increase it and continue to pay attention to only one object or activity. Theoretically, it is possible to concentrate on several activities at the same time, but in practice, the brain is not capable of doing this, and in fact, it jumps back and forth between the topics of concentration without noticing.

When focusing, you direct your concentration to an object or activity and ideally try to experience and recognize this object and activity even more precisely. You direct your mind to explore even more deeply the activity, process, or object. As your focus decreases and you become more superficial, you try to go back to deeper observation.

Focusing and concentrating have overlaps and are similar, like the fact that no one learns it in school and very few people are able to do it successfully. In professional sports, if you can't keep focused on yourself and your goal, you'll have a very hard time being successful. There will be constant influences from outside, other options for training, which will distract the mind and thus the physical strength will decrease.

On the contrary, the one who can keep their concentration and focus will show the best and maximum performance.

Examples of this are countless, but a particularly impressive example are the Shaolin monks who show what is possible with concentration and focus. They create almost superhuman performances through focus and inner balance.

It looks less spectacular when, at today's sporting events, an athlete runs straight from the TV interview to the starting line-up and moments later delivers top performance. However, it requires similar skills and shows the demands of professional sports and the need for mental training in competition to focus on what is important at the moment.

This is not only relevant in competition, but also in training. If you can concentrate intensively on the training before each session, it will improve the quality of the exercises—provided that you keep the necessary calm and relaxed focus. If you take extra breaks during the workout and sharpen your focus, this will further improve your results.

Field Test | Marco Henrichs

Soccer athletics coach Marco Henrichs had adult men and women and U11 junior soccer players move through a defined sequence of exercises. The exercises start with an initial part and time was measured in the following main part.

One group performed the exercise in one stretch and a second group paused for 1–2 seconds to focus before the main part, with the disadvantage of starting the main part without momentum from a standing position.

Result

In the group with the focus pause, a time improvement of 8–10 percent was determined. In addition, the soccer technical execution was evaluated by coaches. This also improved by 10 percent or more compared to the group that had dispensed with the short break.

19.2 Training

19.2.1 Coordination Exercises

The more complex an exercise is, the higher the focus on the exercise must be in order for it to succeed. Complicated exercises are therefore a very good way to train focus. It is helpful if the focus remains or increases during the exercise.

The following method has its charm in the fact that you quickly notice whether and how much you are focused. If you don't manage the stair coordination exercise or if you can actually do it can be a very good indication of your focus level. This becomes especially obvious on the stairs, because the given step length hardly forgives lack of focus.

Exercise Suggestion

1. Start with a simple coordination exercise on the stairs that you know and master. Try to focus on the execution and the movement.

2. Take a more difficult exercise and observe how well and precisely you execute it. After each sequence of exercises, take a short break and reflect on where you focused your attention and how well you kept your focus on the exercise.

3. Increase the difficulty by adding more repetitions, a more difficult exercise, or more speed to the exercise until you fail and have to stop. Notice how you feel, react, and focus your attention, then check how well you were able to keep your concentration on the exercise.

The first part of the reflection is helpful for understanding the next chapter on the topic of setbacks.

19.2.2 Focus on a Task

Focus training is not only possible in sports, but in all areas of life. One possibility is to focus on exactly one activity. This goes against the idea of multi-tasking (i.e., that you can and should do as many things as possible at the same time). By focusing on one activity, such as reading, driving, or exercising, your brain practices functioning in just that way—focused on one activity.

This sounds easy but becomes challenging when you try it practically. Try not to think about or occupy yourself with anything else while driving, cooking, or reading. For almost all people in the Western world, this is an exercise that is difficult even for a few seconds. But the sports principle also applies here: If you practice and train, you will get better.

Noticeable improvements will take time, because the brain of many people is programmed for availability and distraction (i.e., for forms of non-focus). In addition, there is the temptation to do several things at once, with the illusion of getting more done and finishing faster. Those who want to train their brains for peak performance will feel what is possible with a focused mind and what is not possible with an unfocused mind.

Exercise Suggestion

There are activities that work in autopilot mode. Experienced drivers manage to drive from A to B without giving a conscious thought to driving, and this is the ideal exercise to train concentration on an activity. Feel the steering wheel, be aware of your surroundings, decide when to shift gears, brake consciously, and decide when to press the gas pedal.

The same exercise is possible in many activities, such as cooking. You can listen to the radio and talk on the phone, and the routine dish tastes perfect afterwards. To cook this dish consciously, without radio, without phone call, without conversation, and with full focus on each ingredient, each work step, and without wasting a thought on how the dish will taste, whether it will be ready in time, makes the cooking process a completely new experience and begin to train one's own focus power.

19.2.3 Focusing With a Candle

The flickering candle flame provides movement and variety. This makes it easier for people used to television, radio, and reading to focus their attention. Additionally, the fire has a calming effect on body and mind. Because of this easier start, compared to focusing with breathing, you can quickly feel progress in concentration.

Exercise Suggestion

1. Light a candle that burns as quietly as possible and without soot and place it in front of you at a distance of 30–40 cm.

2. Look into the flame and recognize the different colors and movements of the candle.

3. Set an alarm for 30 seconds. During the 30 seconds, pay attention only to the flame and its movement.

4. When you feel that you can focus on the flame of the candle for a larger amount of time, increase the interval.

19.2.4 Focusing With Chocolate

If you want to combine focus training with a tasty snack, you can do this with chocolate. Put a piece of chocolate in your mouth and feel how it slowly melts, notice what flavors you perceive, and everything that happens in your mouth. The important thing is to keep your complete focus and attention on the chocolate. The exercise is about training your strength to focus.

Exercise Suggestion

1. Put a piece of chocolate in your mouth.

2. Observe the chocolate, how it melts, and what flavors develop.

3. Try not to move your tongue while the chocolate melts for several minutes.

4. Sense how it feels when the chocolate is completely melted.

Alternative

This exercise works even better if you use chocolate with whole hazelnuts. This exercise can also be done with many other foods. It works especially well with all types of nuts, as you feel and explore the nut and its shape, taste, and what happens in your mouth.

19.2.5 Focusing With Breathing

A prerequisite to be able to meditate is to focus the mind and thoughts. That is why many masters say they try for 12, 14, or 16 hours a day and only really meditate for a few minutes. It is the challenge par excellence to focus the mind and direct it to a focal object. In many meditation techniques, the breath is used to focus the mind. The goal is to consciously experience as many breaths as possible and to seldom stray with the thoughts.

Exercise Suggestion

1. Breathe deeply through the nose five times and feel the breath as it flows in and out through the nose.

2. Breathe normally through the nose five times without effort, and feel the breath as it flows in and out through the nose.

3. Observe how much you focused on the breath and whether there were thoughts of anything else. If you feel that there were other thoughts and the exercise was rather difficult for you, then start again with the first step. If you find the exercise easy, move on to the next step.

4. Set an alarm for 30 seconds. During the 30 seconds, pay attention only to the breath flowing in and out.

5. Increase the interval when you feel that you can observe your breath for a longer period of time.

Note

This exercise is extremely effective and at the same time it may be difficult or even impossible to do in the first days and weeks. Be patient because it takes time and practice for progress and perfection. If you are unsure how talented you are, ask friends and fellow runners how they do this exercise. This will put your own experience into perspective and, if you have the chance, get other people to practice and share this exercise with.

19.3 Achieve What You Focus On

Everyone knows the self-fulfilling prophecy or the saying, "Energy flows where attention goes."

In disciplines like neurolinguistic programming (NLP) there are numerous methods to program the focus of the conscious and subconscious mind (e.g., with the visualization of goals).

See yourself running across the finish line as a winner—and the likelihood of you experiencing that increases.

What is not trained in this process is focus, which determines how much of one's energy works in the direction of the goal via focus power and what portion of creative power flows into other goals. If these thought flashes are of opposite nature, the path will not be straight to the goal.

That is why training focus—to concentrate on one action, on one goal—makes so much sense. If you run stairs, you can't do anything more meaningful at this time than to focus on just that. This may not always be clear at first glance, because you could also be ruminating about your job, life, etc. On reflection and practice, however, you will find that there are few, if any, exceptions to the benefits of focusing in and on the session. Conversely, it makes little sense to be preoccupied with anything other than yourself, the technique, and the stairs while running stairs.

Focus helps in achieving the goal in a direct way.

Some athletes notice how their cognitive performance decreases during training or after a competition until it seems that the thinking process completely stops and the subconscious, reflexes, and automatisms determine the decisions.

19.4 Focus or Distraction When Running Stairs

There are at least 1,000 things one can think about during a tower run. Whether excuses why the race or workout is going the way it is, or completely different thoughts (e.g., regarding lunch, the job, friends, or the next workout). There is no limit to the creativity of thought but there is to what is possible without focus.

- If you manage to focus your thoughts on yourself, the training, the competition, and your own race, you can be sure to have achieved the best possible result.

- Whoever manages to run past all the what-if thoughts without thinking them through manages to focus their thought power on themselves.

- If you manage not to be distracted by followers, spectators, other people from the organization, or the press, you don't give away any attention or power.

That this can work can be seen in the people who stand at the top of the winners' podiums. One of the reasons, apart from physical performance, why there can only be one winner is that someone else has not managed to focus so well on themselves.

In addition to focusing on oneself, the body, and the race, there is the concept that the athlete distracts himself from the stress and focuses on the scenery, the spectators, or what the situation offers him. Thus, he feels the pain and the load less and can last longer. One of the disadvantages of this is that the body functions and the load are not always observed accurately, and there is a great danger that the athlete will temporarily overexert himself and run too fast.

In stair running in particular, brief excursions into too high of a load range can result in a noticeable drop in performance, and exhaustion increases toward the end of the race. The distraction offered in the stairwell is extremely meager and therefore this technique may be considered for stair runs in nature.

Whether you're an elite athlete or a beginner, the most important thing is to be clear about your goals and needs. Not everyone needs a focus like a laser sword that clears everything out of the way. But with the training on the levels and with the exercise examples here in the chapter, everyone gets effective tools to reach their personal desired level of focus and concentration. This is a process that takes time, strength, and training. The process of focusing and training the power of the mind is very similar and follows similar rules as the process of training the power of the muscles.

20 GOALS AND SETBACKS

An important component for success is setting goals. Think about things like:

• What do I really want to achieve with all my heart, unconditionally?

• What triggers great feelings and euphoria when I just think about it?

• What makes the adrenaline shoot into my body?

These are introductory questions that, among other things, will help you discover how strongly you feel emotionally connected to the goal.

If you've never run a tower run or done stair training, you'll have a hard time imagining what it's like to be the first to cross the finish line. This is easy for a runner who regularly finishes on the podium, and they can emotionally connect with winning and feel the power of victory.

That's why it's important to set a goal that makes your heart beat faster but that is attainable. A goal that is set too high or too low will not tap into this power source of emotional connection.

In addition to this emotional connection with the goal, you can think rationally about the advantages and disadvantages of reaching or not reaching the goal. Both of these techniques can be used in other areas of life outside of sports.

20.1 Goals and Intermediate Goals

Everyone is familiar with the idea of goals and milestones. A big goal is divided into sections. Then a marathon is divided into practical five-kilometer sections or the 91 stories of one of the world's tallest buildings, Taipei 101, are filleted into 10-story blocks each.

Thus, huge and unconquerable distances become manageable in the mind. Strategies can be defined for the respective sections and the focus can be determined.

Why do these strategies not work for all runners?

The answer leads to the crucial details of this technique. At first glance, it seems very easy to divide a race, training, and any other task in life and thus get to the set goal better, easier, and faster. The important thing here is:

- How do you divide the task?

- What do you think consciously and, more importantly, unconsciously?

EXPERT TIP

In the MAINTOWER training building, I have segments and split times for the 10th, 20th, 30th, and 40th floors and the finish at the 52nd floor. Each section has its own characteristics and so my attitude and state of mind changes in the segment. For the last segment from floor 40 to 52, I often give myself the following advice: Ten, eight, five, two more floors, where you can show what you are capable of now.

The somewhat harder verbal pace is expressed in: RUN! If you don't run fast now, then everything you've done so far in training will have been for nothing. This increases the pressure, and when the sentence shoots through the head and body during the last of the three intervals over the 52 floors, it is easy to imagine that the effect is noticeable. The pressure rises.

Detailed Analysis of the Instructions

With positive instruction you achieve a pull effect if you choose it correctly. If the target is too far away, the instruction goes nowhere. A simple example is the following: Put a sheet of paper on the table and move over it very closely with your mouth slightly open. Now try to pull the sheet to your mouth by inhaling. When you are close enough, the sheet lifts off; then try it with a little more distance. This is exactly how the pulling effect works with positive instructions. Correctly chosen, you can take off.

Wrongly chosen, you are too far away from your goals and no matter how deeply you inhale, how loudly you scream at yourself with the positive formulation, you exhaust yourself, but neither the sheet nor you (or your goals) take off.

Complexity of Positive Formulations

1. **Formulation that suits you**

   When you change a single word in a sentence, the sound and energy in it change. That is, what works for you may or may not work for your running mate. The key here is to be highly individual, to try things out, and to gain experience. You will get a feeling for which words, which phrases, and which attitude work well and better for you. A mental trainer, coach, or mentor can help you come up with ideas, test them, and use the additional experience to help you take shortcuts and avoid detours.

   #### 1.1 Appropriate distance
   It's a wonderful idea that anyone can achieve anything, and it turns out that tomorrow's success has a lot to do with today's starting point. One step at a time leads to incredible results over years and decades.

   Use a goal that you can reach with some uncertainty. Whether you need a perceived achievability of 99 percent, 90 percent, or 75 percent is type dependent. The important thing is to be honest with yourself and recognize what you think is realistic. Those who can visualize the sequences of a coordination exercise will implement it sooner or later. If you can't do the exercise in your head, you probably won't get a better result by using your body.

   As with the first point, here it is necessary to be highly individual, to try things out, and to gain experience. You will get a feeling which exercise, training, and competition goals and intermediate goals are suitable (i.e., they are not completely certain to be reached and therefore create an attraction) and thus pull you towards your goal. A mental trainer, coach, or mentor can support you in finding the goals and intermediate goals together with you. Other people can also support you, as they have a different perspective and can feel you and your emotions differently and report this back to you.

2. With a negative instruction, one puts oneself under pressure, one presses the button of fear. You can threaten yourself with the consequences and this is an effective, well-learned mechanism. Almost all actions are based in fear and therefore the brain is used to it and can implement the signal immediately.

The great advantage of the negative formulation is that it does not have to be nearly as individual as the positive formulation. It is more challenging to make a compliment than an insult. Thus, the perceived mental lash becomes a source of strength and performance emerges. Another advantage is that this technique requires minimal to no preparation or forethought. Those who know themselves well can sense which formulation is particularly effective.

Beware of Negative Instructions

This technique is effective and is therefore used by almost every athlete in competitive sports. Even athletes who work with a mental trainer or mental coach can be unconsciously motivated by negative programs. My assumption and experience is that there is almost no exception. The behavioral pattern of avoiding pain and thus doing something out of fear was and is necessary for survival. Doing something out of joy and for good feelings works very well on a superficial level (e.g., good food, nice vacation, buying something great, feelings of happiness, sports, and successes), but underneath the superficial feelings are other drivers.

The negative programs have numerous side effects and one of them is injury, both physical and psychological. Therefore, in sports and in all other areas of life, it makes a lot of sense to work intensively on the topic of focus and goals.

Through focus and concentration you can narrow down the wide spectrum of unconscious thoughts. By setting goals, the thoughts that are then still present are aligned.

20.2 Four-Field Matrix | Eco-Check

Advantage Target achieved	Disadvantage Target achieved
Advantage Target not achieved	Disadvantage Target not achieved

The matrix helps you make decisions and figure out problems that may arise because of the goal.

Answer the questions in each box on a separate sheet of paper. It helps if you number the answers.

For example, I would like to finish the Empire State Building Run-Up in 9:59 | 11:59 | 13:59 minutes. The same applies to a city marathon, which you want to run in under 2:30 | 3:30 | 4:30 hours.

Advantages of Reaching My Goal

1.   I am overjoyed.

2.   I can run with my girlfriend in training afterwards.

3.   I get a finisher medal.

4.   I have a reason to go to a great city.

5.   I get to meet new people at the marathon.

6.   I can show myself how disciplined I can be.

7.   My self-confidence increases.

8.   ....

Disadvantages of Reaching My Goal

1. I need new goals.

2. I have invested a lot of time in training.

3. I do not know what to do then.

4. I felt emptiness.

5. I will want to reach a new goal that is even more ambitious.

Advantages of Not Reaching My Goal

1. I can keep my goal.

2. I don't have to look for even more ambitious goals.

3. I may get encouragement from friends.

4. I can eat chocolate out of frustration.

5. I can feel bad and sorry for myself.

6. I can come up with excuses.

7. I may not have stick with it if I realize it is hopeless earlier.

Disadvantages of Not Reaching My Goal

1. I am disappointed.

2. I may stop running.

3. I have trained for nothing.

4. I have to explain to friends why it didn't work out.

5. I may get self-doubt.

6. I have made myself nervous for nothing.

You can apply this procedure to many decisions and targets in order to better assess which conscious and unconscious effects are related to the target. This is useful because there are goals that are super at first glance, but may bring many problems and disadvantages. Then you may well invest a lot of energy and never reach the goal. This exercise can help to prevent that.

20.3 The Race Is the Same for Everyone (i.e., Advantage of the Underdogs)

As last year's winner, you rarely have an advantage in a race. Expectations of oneself, the organizers, the other runners, and the media are obvious. When an athlete dominates a discipline, the goal of everyone else is clear: overtake and defeat the top star.

• But what is the goal of the top favorite and can he not actually only lose?

This topic will personally concern the fewest runners in pure form, but what is behind it helps everyone. Because while the stars of the scene are struggling with the expectations, every other runner can do their thing without this pressure. They can prepare in peace and without disturbance and save time during interviews. The race itself is then the same length for everyone and so it can happen that someone runs from nowhere to the front with the tailwind of surprise. This experience is great and feels even better.

The important thing is to focus on yourself and not to be irritated by your surroundings. The favorite is not always the one with the best legs. Because the distance is the same for everyone, there is always a chance for surprises—maybe one for you, too.

20.4 Setbacks and Defeats

"Everything happens for a good reason," Giovanni, a Cuban who had fled to the United States, told me a few years ago. He said this when we were talking about the night of his escape, when the raft got caught in a violent storm and was almost completely torn apart; the ocean was pitch black beneath him and he didn't know if there would be a tomorrow.

This is a stunning example, and his attitude is all the more impressive because of it. Granted, he didn't have it at the time, but even with a few years' distance, it seems almost impossible to find the root of his attitude in his near-death experiences, his unimaginably hard and sometimes cruel life—that everything happens for a good reason. With this phrase deeply ingrained, it is easier to endure fatigue fractures, second places, and injury in sports. But besides endurance through relativization, this attitude offers much more for you because it asks you to see the good in the situation. We tend to forget that, and yet it is there.

Deeply hidden, concealed and buried, there is a small part in every tragedy that contains something positive. Every injury brings recovery, relief, change, and distance. Second places motivate, make change easier, and boost training morale. All missed goals have their positive side and seeing that is the art of changing perspective, attitude, and mindset.

It is easier to say that every medal has two sides than to change one's perspective and see the subjects of the supposed dark sides in a different light. Those who manage to do this no longer experience setbacks or defeats, but gain experience.

20.5 Reframing

Reframing gives events a different framework and looks behind the obvious meaning.

Here is a parable from the Chinese Tao.

The Farmer and the Horse

In a poor village lived a farmer. He owned a horse with which he plowed the fields and carried loads. One day the horse ran away. His neighbors shouted how terrible it was, but the farmer only said, "Maybe."

A few days later the horse returned, bringing with it two wild horses. The neighbors all rejoiced at his skill, but the farmer again replied, "Maybe."

The next day, the farmer's son tried to ride one of the wild horses. The horse threw him and he broke both legs. The neighbors all expressed their sympathy to him for this mishap, but from the farmer they again heard only, "Maybe."

The next week, recruiting officers came to the village to take the young men to the army. A war with the neighboring kingdom was brewing. They did not want the farmer's son because his legs were broken. When the neighbors told him how lucky he was, the farmer replied again, "Maybe."

In sports, this change of meaning is often easy and if you can't do it yourself, friends will take care of it. It can also happen when you get supposedly good advice that doesn't suit you. Nevertheless, if you are attentive, you can recognize reframing there.

Second Place at the 2005 Empire State Building Run-Up

On the 74th floor, Rudolf Reitberger, last year's winner, overtook me and secured his second victory at the ESB Run-Up, 320 meters above Manhattan in New York on February 1, 2005.

Of course, I was happy at that moment that I was able to compete right at the front for my first start in New York. But I also felt a strong sense of disappointment that I finished second after 10:24 minutes, which is very often enough to win. One thing you learn in elite sports is that the winner takes it all.

For outsiders, the implications of this sentence are hardly comprehensible, but as an athlete, you quickly notice the difference between the winner and all the other placings. Between the one that ALL are interested in and ALL the others. In some stair races (e.g., in Sydney), there was prize money for the winner and all the others went away empty-handed.

But the other side of the disappointment of that second place was a motivation and clarity that produced a winning subscription over the next seven years from 2006 to 2012. I had learned my lesson and from then on I knew why I was training at every training session.

If it's not clear to me during a session, I ask myself the question: Do I want to finish second? Whatever the training plan says, this question gives me the desire and focus for the upcoming workout. The feeling of coming in second is the ultimate driving force. That's how the road to success started out of defeat. At the time, at the age of 20, I had not yet consciously been aware of this; this realization took a few years.

20.6 There Are No Stairs to Happiness; Happiness Is the Stairs

The quote from Buddha: "There is no way to happiness—happiness is the way", is universally valid and is probably more a guide for life than just for sports and defeats.

It is an attitude that the enlightened monk exemplified 2,500 years ago. It is not the goals and their achievement that make you happy, but the actual doing, the process, and the way to get there.

In sports this means that it is not the victories, not the medals and prize money that make you happy, it is the daily training that makes you happy. It's not the end of the workout when you're in the shower, it's the time before the workout, it's the warm-up, it's the fast intervals, it's the slow breaks, the cool-down and the shower afterwards that make you happy all the time.

- Intellectually it is easy to understand that if every second makes you happy then you are happy. In reality, this attitude is put to the test every second. Who is beaming with joy on floor 80, or during a marathon at kilometer 38, when the thighs and the feet hurt and every kilometer drags?

This idea of constant happiness is thus more of an ideal than a goal achievable by everyone. But if you reach only 10, 30, or 50 percent of that happiness goal, that would be an extraordinarily great life full of many hours filled with overflowing happiness and bliss.

So it's not so much a question of what the goal is, it's much more important that you cultivate that attitude in yourself. One second more of happiness in training, filled with gratitude and joy in doing, is one second further on this way. Finally, the quote reminds us that there is no destination where you can arrive. It is the way to get there that makes you happy.

With this attitude, it is difficult to pursue goals pedantically—to torture oneself falls by the wayside. And yet, it is possible to achieve peak performance.

Why and with what motivation? Because it brings joy to run up stairs quickly, maybe even to you, regardless of whether or not you get a trophy, a tight butt, fancy hips, or praise and recognition.

20.7 Mental Training and Meditation

More and more people are fascinated by the mental power in sports, and in tower running it is crucial to be clearly focused; distracting, disturbing, and performance-reducing thoughts are waiting at every step, in training and in competition. Therefore, mental preparation is part of the overall preparation for a race—the physical training goes hand in hand with the mental. There is a lot of literature and good advice on this if you look beyond your own world and sport, especially if you start reading between the lines of what coaches, trainers, and athletes have to say.

20.8 Meditate Like Buddha

In 2019, I went to a meditation center in Sri Lanka where I attended a 10-day course in the meditation technique that Siddhartha Gautama—many know him as Buddha—had recognized.

It felt like a training camp for the mind. Anyone who has heard of Vipassana knows that it is also a physical challenge to practice meditation from early in the morning until late at night. Every day, I sat on the floor and meditated for over 10 hours.

Often at that time I wondered how I was going to get through that. This question already didn't help in any staircase and that's why I knew what to do—keep running or in that case stay seated and follow the teacher's instructions.

Central elements in meditation are equanimity and focus, and this is also true for stair running. If you start fighting the stairs, cursing the ascent and your own decisions, you will fight a grueling battle to the finish. If you manage to smile over or push away the physical sensations—mostly intense pain—you can more calmly pant up the stair chute.

But in the process, of course, you make fun of yourself, and that comes at a price. The bill comes in the form of injury or failure that can't be explained. Through social media and interviews, it's easy and obvious for athletes to read about and follow—the cycle of success and defeat, of rise and fall, the interplay we know from everywhere—day and night, ebb and flow.

REFERENCES

Tactics in Skyscraper Running
Minetti, A.E., D. Cazzola, E. Seminati, M. Giacometti, G.S. Roi. 2011. "Skyscraper running: physiological and biomechanical profile of a novel sport activity. Scandinavian Journal of Medicine & Science in Sports, Volume 21, Issue 2, pp. 293–301.

Static and Dynamic Stretching
Faelli, Emanuela, Piero Ruggeri, Marco Panascì, Vittoria Ferrando, Ambra Bisio, Luca Filipas, and Marco Bove. 2021. "The Effect of Static and Dynamic Stretching During Warm-Up on Running Economy and Perception of Effort in Recreational Endurance Runners." International Journal of Environmental Research and Public Health, 18.

Effect of Compression Stockings in Sports
Allaert, F.A., C. Gardon-Mollard, J.P. Benigni. 2011. "Effet d'une compression élastique de classe II française (18 - 21 mmHg) sur l'adaptationmusculaire à l'effort et la récupération des marathoniens." Phlébologie, 64(4), 57–62.

Changes and Differences in Men and Women in Stair Running
Stark, Daniel, Stefania Di Gangi, Caio Victor Sousa, Pantelis Nikolaidis, Beat Knechtle. 2020. "Tower Running-Participation, Performance Trends, and Sex Difference." International Journal of Environmental Research and Public Health, 17(6), 1902.

Performance Climbing With Stair Sprinting
Jenkins, E. Madison, Leah N. Nairn, Lauren E. Skelly, Jonathan P. Little, and Martin J. Gibala. 2019. "Do stair climbing exercise 'snacks' improve cardiorespiratory fitness?" Applied Physiology, Nutrition, and Metabolism, 44 (6), 681–684.

Credits

Cover photo, interior photos, and videos: Moritz Schleiffelder | heymo-studio.de

Other photos:

P. 13 left: Sporting Republic/ISF Vertical World Circuit

P. 13 right, 23, 27, 37, 53, 80, 81, 167, 168, 170: Thomas Dold

P. 38: New York Road Runner's Club

P. 45: Dr. Sascha Härtel - KIT University Karlsruhe

P. 57–64: Marcel Meister (Maintower)

P. 78: AOK Baden-Württemberg

p. 162, 175 (Ecotrail Paris/La Verticale de la Tour Eiffel), 177, 180: Suzy Walsham

p. 163: Tomasz Klinsz

P. 164: Verena Fink

P. 178: Vertical World Circuit

P. 231: Thomas Niedermüller

P. 233: Sporting Republic/ISF Vertical World Circuit

Cover design: Anja Elsen

Interior design: Annika Naas, Anja Elsen

Layout: DiTech Publishing Services, www.ditechpubs.com

Managing editor: Elizabeth Evans

Copy editor: Anne Rumery

Thomas Dold

COACH · SPEAKER · WORLD CHAMPION

find **your** way.

What do you want more or less of in life?
What decisions do you have to make?
What makes you happy?

- Keynotes
- Mentoring
- Coaching

know **thyself**

www.thomasdold.com